Jokes for All Occasions

（美）Edward J. Clode \编
亢海宏 张颖 \译

● 英汉对照

幽 默
的艺术

百花文艺出版社
BAIHUA LITERATURE AND
ART PUBLISHING HOUSE

图书在版编目（CIP）数据

幽默的艺术：英汉对照/（美）克洛德（Clode,E）编著；亢海宏，张颖译. —天津：百花文艺出版社，2009.1（2012.7重印）

ISBN 978-7-5306-5150-6

Ⅰ.幽… Ⅱ.①克…②亢…③张… Ⅲ.①英语—汉语—对照读物②笑话—作品集—世界 Ⅳ.H319.4：I

中国版本图书馆CIP数据核字(2009)第000886号

百花文艺出版社出版发行
地址：天津市和平区西康路35号
邮编：300051
e-mail:bhpubl@public.tpt.tj.cn
http://www.bhpubl.com.cn
发行部电话：(022)23332651 邮购部电话：(022)27695043
全国新华书店经销
天津泰宇印务有限公司印刷
*
开本880×1230毫米 1/32 印张8.25 插页2 字数160千字
2009年4月第1版 2012年7月第3次印刷
印数：8001-11000册 定价：18.00元

◉幽默是魔法棒

可以化解悲伤，冷却狂喜，点醒愚钝

◉幽默是智慧

教你从另一个角度看待生活和人性

目录

Contents

1. 大千世界

What a Wonderful World!

(1)

The raw Irishman was told by the farmer for whom he worked that the pumpkins in the corn patch were mule´s eggs, which only needed someone to sit on them to hatch. He was ambitious to own a mule, and, selecting a large pumpkin, he sat on it industriously every moment he could steal from his work. Came a day when he grew impatient, and determined to hasten the hatching. He stamped on the pumpkin. As it broke open, a startled rabbit broke from its cover in an adjacent corn shock and scurried across the field. Pat chased it, shouting:

"Hi, thou! Stop! Don´t you know your own father?"

有一个新来乍到的爱尔兰人，去给一个农场主打工。农场主告诉他玉米地里的南瓜是骡子蛋，只要有人坐在上面，就可以孵出小骡子来。爱尔兰人很想要一头骡子，于是，就挑了一个大个儿南瓜，一有空闲，就坐在上面孵。终于有一天，他有点儿不耐烦了，决定加快孵化的进程。他用力踩了一下南瓜，结果，玉米地一阵颤动，南瓜裂开了，一只受了惊吓的兔子从藏着的地方跳了出来，一蹦一跳地穿过玉米地，跑远了。帕特在后面，一边追，一边喊：

"喂，你！站住！你连自己的爸爸都不认了？"

(2)

The clergyman drew near to the baptismal font, and directed that the candidates for baptism should now be presented. A woman in the congregation gave a gasp of dismay and turned to her husband, whom she addressed in a strenuous whisper:

"There! I just knew we´d forget something. John, you run right home as fast as you can, and fetch the baby."

牧师走到洗礼盘前，说可以把即将接受洗礼的孩子带过来了。人群中的一位妇女惊呼了一声，转身焦急地低声对丈夫说："糟了！我刚才就觉得我们好像忘了什么。约翰，赶紧回去，越快越好，把孩子抱来。"

(3)

The raw recruit was on sentry duty. He had a piece of pie, which he had brought from the canteen, and proceeded to enjoy it. Just then, the colonel happened along, and scowled at the sentry, who paid no attention to him whatever.

"Do you know who I am?" the officer demanded.

The sentry shook his head. "Maybe, the veterinarian, or the barber, or mebby the colonel himself." The sentry laughed loudly at his own wit. But he withered as the officer sternly declared his identity.

"Oh good land!" the recruit cried out in consternation. "Please, hold this pie while I present arms."

新入伍的士兵在站岗，手里拿着从餐厅带出来的馅儿饼。正当他打算好好享用的时候，上校碰巧路过，他看着哨兵皱起了眉头，可是哨兵对此却毫无察觉。

"你知道我是谁吗？"上校问道。

哨兵摇摇头。"可能是兽医，或者是理发师，也许是上校。"

哨兵觉得自己的回答很机智，不由得笑出了声。可是，当上校报出自己的真实身份时，哨兵立刻惊慌失措。

"我的妈呀，请帮我拿着馅儿饼，我好向您致举枪礼。"

(4)

Specialist (to patient suffering from insomnia): "And did you try my plan of counting sheep coming through a gate?"

Patient: "Well, I counted up to a hundred and twenty thousand and thirty-nine, and then it was time to get up."

医生(对患失眠症的病人)说:"我不是让你数羊了吗?你数了没有?"

病人:"我数了，可是等我数到十二万零三十九只羊的时候,就该起床了。"

(5)

"I´m so glad to see you. And how did you enjoy your visit to the South?"

"Oh, not very much! There wasn´t a soul where I was staying except intimate friends."

"很高兴见到你。你在南方过得愉快吧?"

"噢,不太愉快!我待的那个地方,除了熟人,还是熟人。"

（6）

"They say that she was his stenographer before marriage."

"She has evidently reversed the order of things."

"How so?"

"She does the dictating now."

"听说结婚前她是他的速记员。"

"那么，很显然，她现在是反其道而行之了。"

"怎么回事？"

"因为她现在只做口述。"

（7）

Ability to look on two sides of a question is usually a virtue, but it may degenerate into a vice. Thus, a visitor found his bachelor friend glumly studying an evening waistcoat. When inquiry was made, this explanation was forthcoming:

"It´s quite too soiled to wear, but really, it´s not dirty enough to go to the laundry. I can´t make up my mind just what I should do about it."

能够一分为二地看待问题通常是一种美德。但同时，也可以沦落为一个人的缺陷。一位客人发现他的单身汉朋友正在对着一件晚礼服发愁。在他的再三询问下，朋友才作了如下的解释：

“这件衣服脏得不能穿了，可是，还没有脏到要拿去洗的地步。我不知道拿它怎么办。”

(8)

The highly efficient housewife bragged that she always rose early, and had every bed in the house made before anybody else in the house was up.

一位做事效率很高的家庭主妇自夸说，她起床总是很早，而且总是在家人起床之前，就整理完了所有的床铺。

(9)

The optimist fell from the top story of a skyscraper. As he passed the fourth story, he was overheard muttering:

“So far, so good!”

有个乐天派从摩天大楼的顶层掉了下来。到

第四层的时候，人们还听到他自言自语：

“到目前为止，还不错！”

(10)

The lady who had some culture, but not too much, was describing the adventure of her husband, who had been in Messina at the time of the earthquake.

"It was awful," she declared, in tense tones. "When Jim went to bed, everything was perfectly quiet. And then, when he woke up, all of a sudden, there beside him was a yawning abbess!"

一个有点儿文化，但是水平并不高的女人这样描述其丈夫在墨西拿地震中遇险的情形。

“太可怕了，”她语气中充满了惊恐。“吉姆上床睡觉的时候，一切都安静极了，可是，醒来的时候，突然发现，身旁躺着一个修女，而且还在打哈欠。”

(11)

The young mother asked the man who supplied her with milk if he kept any calves, and smiled pleasedly when he said that he did.

"Then," she continued brightly, "bring me a pint of calf's milk every day. I think cow's milk is too strong for baby."

年轻的母亲问给她送牛奶的人家里有没有小牛犊。听送奶人说有，年轻的母亲不禁喜上眉梢，欢快地说：

"那你以后每天都给我送一品脱小牛犊的奶吧。我觉得母牛的奶婴儿喝着太浓了。"

(12)

The Japanese are remarkably tidy in the matter of floors. They even remove their shoes at the doorway. A Japanese student in New York was continually distressed by the dirty hallways of the building in which he lived. In the autumn, the janitor placed a notice at the entrance, which read:

"Please wipe your feet."

The Japanese wrote beneath in pencil:

"On going out."

日本人非常重视地板的洁净，他们甚至要把鞋脱在门口。一个在纽约上学的日本学生因为宿舍地板很脏而备感痛苦。秋天的时候，看门人在入口处贴了一个告示：

"请在门口擦擦鞋。"

日本学生用铅笔又在下面添了以下内容：

"出门的时候。"

（13）

The day laborer was of a cheerful disposition that naturally inclined to seek out the good in every situation. He was a genuine optimist. Thus, after tramping the three miles from home to begin the day's work on the ditch, he discovered that he had been careless, and explained to a fellow laborer:

"I've gone and done it now! I left my lunch at home."

Then, suddenly he beamed happily, as he added:

"And it's a good thing I did, for the matter of that, because I left my teeth at home, too."

有一个打工仔，天性乐观，任何事情总是往好处想。有一次，从家里步行三英里去挖水沟，到那儿才发现自己粗心大意，忘带东西了，他对工友说：

“天哪，我忘了带午饭了。”

可是，转眼之间，他又兴高采烈地说：

“不过，幸亏如此，因为我也忘了带我的假牙了。”

(14)

First Burglar: “Say, Bill, the doctor who fixed the leg I broke doing that second-story job didn´t do a thing but soak me fifty plunks!”

Second Burglar: “Oh, say, wasn´t that robbery?”

第一个入室抢劫的盗贼：“哎，比尔，上次做二楼那个活儿的时候，我不是把腿摔断了吗？那个给我看腿的医生什么都没做，就要了我50张票子！”

第二个入室抢劫的盗贼：“啊，我说，这不是抢劫吗？”

(15)

She: "What made George and Alice break their engagement?"

He: "He complained that she was too´Effeminate´ for the present day."

她:"为什么乔治和爱丽丝解除了婚约?"

他:"他觉得她太女人气了,不符合潮流。"

(16)

John: "You wait here, Mirandy, while I buy your ticket."

Mirandy: "Don´t you do it, John; you can´t say for sure that the train will show up–I never believe in paying for a thing till I get it."

约翰:"在这里等我，梅兰蒂，我去给你买票。"

梅兰蒂:"别买了,约翰。也不知道火车会不会来——在没有拿到东西之前最好别付钱。"

(17)

Steward: Can I do anything for you, sir?

Passenger (faintly): You might present my compliments to the chief engineer and ask him if there is any hope of the boilers blowing up.

航空小姐：我能为您效劳吗？

乘客（虚弱地）：请您替我向总机械师致意，顺便问问他锅炉是不是有可能爆炸。

(18)

Pat was a simple country yokel who had never strayed from the outskirts of his native village, and because he stood in a railway station for the first time of his life, his amazement was great.

The vastness of his surroundings completely dazzled him, but when the 330 express dashed through the station, that did it. He kept his eyes glued on the tunnel through which it had disappeared, staring after it as though some kind of miracle had happened. He remained like this for several minutes, much to the amusement of the onlookers, until at length an inquisitive porter asked him what he was staring at.

"I was just thinking," he said, pulling himself together, "what a terrible smash there would have been if he´d a missed the hole!"

帕特是一个乡下人，他从来没有离开过自己的村庄。因此当他有生以来第一次来到火车站时，他的惊异可想而知。

火车站的环境让他眼花缭乱，当 330 次快速列车驶冲过车站的时候，他更是目瞪口呆。列车进入隧道消失之后，他的眼睛仍然紧紧盯着隧道，对他来说这一切简直不可思议。他就这样目不转睛地盯着隧道看了好几分钟，最后连旁观的人都觉得好奇，有一个搬运工忍不住问他在看什么。

"我在想，"他好不容易回过神来。"要是火车没有对准那个洞口，那岂不是要被撞成碎片了！"

(19)

An old black man visited a doctor and received instructions as to what he should do. Shaking his head, he was about to leave the office, when the doctor called out "Hey, there, uncle, you forgot to pay me." "Pay you for what, sir?" "For my advice." "No, sir," said the black man, shuffling out. "I´ve considered it from all angles and decided not to take it."

一位年老的黑人去看病，医生给了他一些建

议。他摇摇头，正打算离开的时候，医生冲他喊道：“喂，大叔，您忘了付钱了。”“付什么钱啊？”“我的建议钱啊。”“哦，先生，”老人慢吞吞地说，“我左思右想，还是决定不采纳你的建议了。”

(20)

The boy who had "made good" in town asked his old mother to come to London. He gave the old lady the best room in the hotel—one with a private bath adjoining. The next morning the boy asked:

"Did you have a good night's rest?"

"Well, no, I didn't," she replied. "The room was all right, and the bed was pretty. But I couldn't sleep very much, for I was afraid someone would want to take a bath, and the only way to it was through my room!"

有个小伙子在伦敦混得不错，于是把他的老母亲接了过来，并安排老人住在饭店最好的房间里，因为那个房间带浴室。第二天早晨，小伙子问：

“昨晚您睡得好吗？”

“噢，不，不好。房间很好，床也不错，可是我没怎么睡，总担心有人要洗澡，要知道到澡堂必须经过我的房间。”

(21)

Doctor (at door, to butler): "Tell your master the doctor is here."

Butler: "The master is in great pain, sir. He is receiving nobody."

医生（在门口，对男管家）："告诉你家主人医生到了。"

男管家："主人正在生病，先生。他谁也不想见。"

(22)

The old mountaineer and his wife arrived at a railway station, and for the first time in their lives beheld a train of cars, which was standing there. The husband looked the engine over very carefully, and shook his head.

"Well, what do you think of it, father?" asked the old lady.

"She´ll never start," was the firm answer: "she´ll never start."

The conductor waved, the bell rang, the locomotive puffed, the train moved slowly at first, then faster. It was disappearing in the distance when the wife inquired slyly:

"Well, pa, what do you think of it now?"

The old man shook his head more

violently than before.

"She'll never stop," he asserted; "she'll never stop!"

一位老山民和他的老婆来到一个火车站，生平第一次看到火车。火车正停靠在站上。老头儿来回仔细看了火车好半天，摇了摇头。

"你觉得怎么样，孩子他爸？"老妇人问。

"它绝对不会动的，绝对不会。"山民不容置疑地回答。

可是，随着列车长的指挥，和一声铃响，机车喷出黑烟，开始徐徐启动，接着跑得越来越快，最后消失在远处，老婆带着怪腔又问：

"孩子他爸，这下你觉得怎样？"

老头儿还是摇了摇头，比上次还要不容置疑地回答：

"它绝对不会停的，绝对不会。"

(23)

He was a stout man, and his feet were big in proportion. He wore stout boots, too, with broad, square, sensibly-shaped toes; and when he came into the boot shop to buy another pair, he found he had some difficulty in getting what he wanted.

A dozen, two dozen, three dozen pairs were brought and shown him.

"No, no! Square toes—must have square toes," he insisted.

"But, sir, everybody is wearing shoes with pointed toes. They are fashionable this season."

"I´m sorry," said the stout man gravely, as he got up and prepared to leave the shop. "I´m very sorry to have troubled you, I´m sure. But, you see, I´m still wearing my last season´s feet!"

他是一个身材高大的人，脚也很大，他的脚趾又宽又长也很大，他得穿很大的皮靴。因此，当他去皮靴店想再买一双靴子的时候，他发现很难买到他想要的皮靴。

店员拿出一打又一打靴子让他看，足足拿出了三打。

"不行，不行！必须是方头的。"他坚持。

"可是，先生，现在大家都穿尖头的。今年流行尖头皮鞋。"

"对不起，"魁梧的男人认真地说。他起身，准备离开。"很抱歉给您添麻烦了。可是，你看，我的脚还是去年流行的样式。"

(24)

"Look here," began the youth, as he entered a butcher´s shop, and displayed two lovely-looking black-and-blue eyes, "you have fresh beef for sale?"

"I have," responded the butcher.

"And fresh beef is good for black eyes, is it not?"

"It is."

"Very well. I have the eyes, you have the beef. Do you think you can sell me a pound or so without asking how I got ornamented?"

"I´ll do my best, sir."

The butcher cut off the meat, and received his money without another look at his customer. At the last moment, however, the old Adam proved too strong for him.

"Look here," he said, handing back the cash, "I´ll make you a present of the beef. Now tell me all about the fight."

一个两眼青紫得有点儿好玩的年轻人走进肉店说:"喂,有新鲜牛肉吗?"

"有呀,"肉店老板说。

"牛肉可以治乌青眼,对吧?"

"是的。"

"那好。别管我的眼睛,你只管卖你的牛肉。你能不能卖给我一磅左右的牛肉,但不要问我的眼睛是怎么弄成这个样子的?"

"我尽力吧,先生。"

肉店老板切了一块牛肉，接过了肉钱，没有再看他的顾客。可是，在最后一刻，人类的本性还是占了上风。

“喂，”肉店老板把钱递了回去。“牛肉就算我送你的吧。告诉我你怎么打成这个样子的。”

（25）

“Yes,” proudly announced the ex-captain, who is manager of a new seaside hotel, “all our employees are former Service men, every one of them. The reception clerk is an old infantry man, the waiters have all been non-coms, the chef was a mess-sergeant, the house doctor was a base hospital surgeon, the house-detective was an intelligence man; even the pages were cadets.”

“And have you any former military police?” he was asked.

“Yes,” he replied joyously. “When there´s a good stiff wind blowing we set them to clean the outsides of the windows on the eighth floor!”

“是的，”已经退伍的陆军上尉说，他现在已经是一家新开的海滨饭店的经理。

“我们的员工都是退伍军人，所有的人都是。

接待员是一个老步兵，厨师以前是司务长，常驻医生是基地医院的外科医生，常驻警员以前是情报员，甚至连跑堂的都是军校毕业的。”

“那么你们的雇员中有没有退伍的宪兵？”

“有呀，”他快活地回答。“如果刮大风，我们会派他们去擦八层楼的外窗。”

(26)

“Tell me, does your husband snore?”

“Oh, yes, indeed—so delightfully.”

“What?”

“Yes, really—he´s so musical you know, his voice is baritone, he only snores operatic bits, mostly Aida.”

“你丈夫打鼾吗？”

“当然，他的鼾声非常悦耳。”

“什么？”

“真的，你知道，我丈夫很有乐感。他天生一副男中音的嗓子，他的鼾声就是歌剧，大多数时候他唱的是《阿伊达》。”

(注：意大利作曲家G·威尔第创作的4幕歌剧，举世公认的十大经典歌剧之一。)

(27)

The clergyman was calling, when the youthful son and heir approached his mother proudly, and exhibited a dead rat. As she shrank in repugnance, he attempted to reassure her:

"Oh, it´s dead all right, mama. We beat it and beat it and beat it, and it´s deader ´n dead."

His eyes fell on the clergyman, and he felt that something more was due to that reverend presence. So he continued in a tone of solemnity:

"Yes, we beat it and beat it until—until God called it home!"

教士来家访，正在这时，年幼的儿子，也是这家的继承人，走到妈妈面前，得意地拿出一只死耗子给妈妈看。妈妈惊恐地往后退去，儿子却安慰她道：

"噢，它已经死了。我们打它，打呀打呀，现在它已经死死的了。"

这时，他看见了教士，觉得应该表现一番，于是，他语气凝重地说：

"是的，我们打它，打呀打呀，一直把它打到上帝那儿去了。"

2. 实话实说

Tell It as It Is

(28)

An excellent old gentleman grew hard of hearing, and was beset with apprehension lest he become totally deaf. One day, as he rested on a park bench, another elderly citizen seated himself alongside. The apprehensive old gentleman saw that the new comer was talking rapidly, but his ears caught no faintest sound of the other's voice. He listened intently–in vain. He cupped a hand to his ear, but there was only silence. At last, in despair, he spoke his thought aloud:

"It's come at last! I know you've been talking all this while, but I haven't heard a single word."

The answer, given with a grin, was explicit and satisfying to the worried deaf man:

"I hain't been talkin'—jest a-chewin'."

一位老绅士的听力越来越差，他非常担心耳朵会完全变聋。一天，他在公园的长椅上休息，这时，另一位老人过来坐在了他的旁边。担心自己耳朵变聋的老人看到新来的老人正在快速地说着什么，可是，他却一点儿声音都没听到。他仔细去听，但还是什么也听不见。他用双手拢住耳朵去听，还是一点声音也没有。最后，他绝望地高声问道：

“这一天还是到了。我知道你一直在说话，可是我却一个字也听不见。”

那位老人咧开嘴笑了，他清清楚楚的回答令担心耳聋的老人如释重负：

“刚才我根本没说话，我一直在嚼口香糖。”

（29）

When a certain officer of the governor´s staff died, there were many applicants for the post, and some were indecently impatient. While the dead colonel was awaiting burial, one aspirant buttonholed the governor, asking:

“Would you object to my taking the place of the colonel?”

“Not at all,” the governor replied tartly. “See the undertaker.”

一位长官的手下死了。许多人想填补空缺，有些人为了得到空缺甚至连体面都不顾了。在死者等待下葬之时，一位当官心切的人拉住长官问：

“由我来代替他的位置，您不反对吧？”

“当然不，”长官直接回答，“去找殡仪师吧。”

（30）

At a reception the woman chatted for some time with the distinguished man of learning, and displayed such intelligence that one of the listeners complimented her.

“Oh, really,” she said with a smile, “I´ve just been concealing my ignorance.”

The professor spoke gallantly.

“Not at all, not at all, my dear madam! Quite the contrary, I do assure you.”

招待会上，一位女士与一位学识渊博的教授交谈了一会儿。交谈中，她表现出的智慧受到了在座一位聆听者的赞赏。

“哪里，哪里”她谦虚地笑着说，“其实刚才我一直在掩盖我的无知呢。”

教授殷勤地接口道：“哪里，哪里，亲爱的夫人！一点也没掩盖，对此我深信不疑。”

(31)

We are more particular nowadays about cleanliness than were those of a past generation. Charles Lamb, during a whist game, remarked to his partner:

"Martin, if dirt were trumps, what a hand you'd have!"

对于清白,我们这一代人比上一代人更挑剔。

查尔斯·兰姆,在玩扑克牌的时候,对他的搭档说:

"马丁,如果肮脏就是耍手段的话,你可真算是高手了!"

(32)

A victim of chronic bronchitis called on a well-known physician to be examined. The doctor, after careful questioning, assured the patient that the ailment would respond readily to treatment.

"You're so sure," the sufferer inquired, "I suppose you must have had a great deal of experience with this disease."

The physician smiled wisely, and answered in a most confidential manner:

"Why, my dear sir, I've had bronchitis

myself for more than fifteen years."

一个慢性气管炎病人到一个有名的医生那里去看病。医生仔细询问过病情之后，向病人打包票说他的这点儿小病很快就会好转。

病人说："您这么肯定，我想您对这种病的治疗一定很有经验吧？"

医生莞尔一笑，非常自信地回答道：

"怎么，不相信？我自己得的就是气管炎，至少有15年了。"

（33）

A woman visitor to the city entered a taxicab. No sooner was the door closed than the car leaped forward violently, and afterward went racing wildly along the street, narrowly missing collision with innumerable things. The passenger, naturally enough, was terrified. She thrust her head through the open window of the door, and shouted at the chauffeur:

"Please, be careful, sir! I´m nervous. This is the first time I ever rode in a taxi."

The driver yelled in reply, without turning his head:

"That´s all right, ma´am. It´s the first time I ever drove one!

一位刚进城的妇女上了一辆出租车。门还没关好，车就猛地向前冲去，然后，在街上横冲直撞。女乘客吓坏了。她冲着司机大喊：

“先生，请您小心点儿！我有点儿害怕。这是我第一次坐出租。”

司机头也不回地大声安慰道：

“不要紧，夫人，我也是第一次开出租。”

(34)

The Southern planter heard a commotion in his poultry house late at night. With shot gun in hand, he made his way to the door, flung it open and curtly ordered:

"Come out of there, you ornery thief!"

There was silence for a few seconds, except for the startled clucking of the fowls. Then a heavy bass voice boomed out of the darkness:

"Please, Colonel, dey ain´t nobody here ´cept jes´ us chickens!"

夜半时分，一个南方的种植园主听到他家的鸡舍里一阵骚乱。于是，他拿起猎枪，来到鸡舍前，一脚踢开门，厉声喝道：

“滚出来，你这个臭贼！”

没有回答，只有鸡群受到惊吓后咯咯的叫声。过了一会儿，黑暗中传来一个瓮声瓮气的声音：

“上校先生，这里除了俺们这些鸡，没别人！

(35)

The meditative Hollander delivered a monologue to his dog:

“You are only a dog, but I wish I were you. When you go your bed in, you should turn round tree times and lie down; when I go de bed in, I have to lock up the block, and wind up de clock, and put out de cat, and undress myself, and my wife wakes up and scolds, and den de baby wakes and cries and I have to walk him de house around, and den maybe I get myself to bed in time to get up again.”

“When you get up you should stretch yourself, dig your neck a little, and you are up. I have to light the fire, put on de kettle, scrap some wheat for my wife, and get myself breakfast. You be lays round all day and have plenty of fun. I have to work all day and have plenty of trouble. When you die, you vas dead; when I die, I have to go somewhere again.”

有一位好思考的荷兰人对他的狗说了下面这一番话：

“虽然你只是一条狗，可是，我真想变成你。你睡觉前，转三圈躺下就行了。可是我呢，睡觉前得锁大门，上闹钟，把猫放到房间外面，脱衣服。老婆醒了还要训斥我，孩子醒了要哭，所以我得抱着孩子在屋里转来转去地哄，等我终于可以睡觉的时候，就又该起床了。”

“你起床的时候，只要伸伸腰，挠挠脖子就行了。可是我呢，我得生火，烧开水，为我老婆做早饭，然后我自己吃早饭。你呢，整天这里躺躺，那里躺躺，而且乐趣多多。可是我呢，整天都要干活，而且麻烦不断。你死了就死了。可我死了，还得搬去另外一个地方。”

（36）

After a trip abroad, a lady inquired of her colored washerwoman:

“Lucy, do you and your husband quarrel now the same as you used to?”

“No, indeed, ma′am,” was the reply.

“That is good. I′m sure you′re very glad of it, aren′t you?”

“Ah sho′ly is.”

“What caused you to stop quarreling,

Lucy?" the lady asked.

The explanation was simple and sufficient: "He died."

从国外旅游回来，女主人问女佣：

"露西，你和你丈夫还吵架吗？"

"不吵了，夫人。"女佣回答。

"这就好。你现在肯定很高兴吧？"

"当然了。"

"那么你们怎么就不再吵了呢？"女主人问。

女佣的理由既简单又充分：

"他死了。"

(37)

One of the New York churches is notorious for its exclusiveness. A colored man took a fancy to the church, and promptly told the minister that he wished to join. The clergyman sought to evade the issue by suggesting to the man that he reflect more carefully on the matter, and make it the subject of prayers for guidance. The following day, the dark encountered the minister.

"I have prayed, sir," he declared, beaming, "and the Lord he has sent me an answer last night."

"And what was it?" queried the clergyman, somewhat at a loss. "What did the Lord say?"

"Well, sir, He has asked me what church I wanted to join, and I told Him it was yours . And he says: ′Ho, ho, that church!′ says he. ′You can′t get in there. I know you can′t—′cause I have been trying to get in that church for ten years myself and I couldn′t!′"

纽约有一个教堂因为排外而臭名昭著。一个黑人喜欢上了那个教堂，立刻找到神父说他希望加入。为了打发他走，神父说让他再认真考虑考虑，最好祈祷听听上帝的意见。第二天，黑人遇到了神父。他兴高采烈地说，"我祈祷了。昨天晚上，主已经给了我答案。"

"噢？答案是什么？主怎么说？"神父将信将疑地问道。"主问我想加入哪个教堂，我就告诉他是您的那个教堂。主说，'原来是那个教堂！你不能去那里。我知道你去不了那里，因为十年来，我也一直想去那个教堂，可是却去不了'。"

（38）

An Irishman on a scaffolding four stories high heard the noon whistle. But when he would have descended, he found that the ladder had been removed. One of his fellow workmen on the pavement below, to whom he called, explained that the foreman had carried off the ladder for another job.

"But how'll I get down?" Pat demanded.

Mike, on the pavement, suggested jumping as the only means. Pat's lunch was below, he was hungry, and he accepted the suggestion seriously.

"Will you catch me?" he demanded.

"Sure, an' I'll do that," Mike agreed.

Pat clapped his arms in imitation of a rooster, and crowed, to bolster up his courage, and leaped. He regained consciousness after a short interval, and feebly sat up on the pavement. He regarded Mike reproachfully.

"For why did you not catch me?" he asked, and the pain in bones sounded in his voice.

"Sorry," Mike replied sympathetically, "I was waiting for you to bounce!"

派特在四层高的脚手架上干活，听到中午休息的哨声他打算下来，可是却发现梯子不见了。下面小路上的工友麦克告诉他梯子被搬到别处去用了。

"那我怎么下来？"派特喊道。

麦克建议说只有跳下来了。派特实在是饿了，午饭眼睁睁就在下面，派特忍不住把麦克的建议当了真。

"你能接住我吗？"他问麦克。

"当然，没问题。"麦克回答。

为了壮胆，派特张开两臂，像公鸡那样上下拍打了几下，还模仿公鸡叫了几声，然后就跳了下来。

过了好一会儿，派特才清醒过来。他有气无力地坐起来，看着麦克，忍着浑身骨头的疼痛，责备道：

"你为什么不接我呢？"

"对不起，"麦克不无同情地说，"我本来是想等你弹起来再接的。"

(39)

The old gentleman was lost in a London fog, so thick that he could hardly see his hand before his face. He became seriously alarmed when he found himself in a slimy alley. Then he heard footsteps approaching through the obscurity, and sighed with relief.

"Where am I going to?" he cried anxiously.

A voice replied weirdly from the darkness beyond:

"Into the river—I´ve just come out!"

一位老绅士在伦敦伸手不见五指的浓雾中迷了路。惊愕之中，他来到一条泥泞的小道上。这时他听到迷雾中传来脚步声，于是如释重负地长出一口气，焦急地喊道：

“这是到哪里去的路？”

一个古怪的声音从远处的黑暗中传了过来：

“河里——我刚从那里出来！”

（40）

Parent: “I should like you to have ´good´ in your report, and not always ´fair.´”

Young Hopeful: “I dare say you would, Dad. But, you see, I´m an ordinary boy of ordinary parents, and that´s an ordinary report.”

望子成龙的父母：“我希望你在报告中不要总是用‘差不多’，应该多用点‘好’。”

未来的龙：“爸爸，这是你的愿望而已。不过，你知道，我是一个普通的男孩儿，父母也是普通人，而这个报告也是一个普通的报告。”

(41)

Employer: "John, I wish you wouldn't whistle at your work."

Boy: "I wasn't working, Sir; only whistling."

老板："约翰，我希望你干活儿的时候不要吹口哨。"

男孩儿："先生，我没干活，我只是在吹口哨。"

(42)

The Arctic explorer at a reception on his return gave an informal talk concerning his experiences. He explained that a point further north would have been reached, if the dogs had not given out at a critical time.

A lady, who had followed the explorer's remarks carefully, ventured a comment as the speaker paused:

"But I thought those Esquimaux dogs were actually tireless."

The explorer hesitated, and cleared his throat before answering.

"I spoke," he elucidated, "in a—er—culinary sense."

一位从北极回来的探险家在回来的招待会上讲起了他的经历。他解释说，如果不是那些狗在关键时刻实在不行了，探险队员可以再往北走一点。

一位女士在很认真地听他讲，当他停顿下来的时候，女士小心翼翼地说道：

“可是，那些爱斯基摩狗不是永不疲倦的吗？”

探险者犹豫了一下，清了清嗓子，然后解释道：

“我所说的不行了，是从营养价值上讲的。”

(43)

The clergyman on his vacation wrote a long letter concerning his traveling experiences to be circulated among the members of the congregation. The letter opened in this form:

“Dear Friends:

“I will not address you as ladies and gentlemen, because I know you so well.”

一位外出度假的教士写了一封长信，想让他的教友们在集会时相互传阅了解他的行程。信是这样开始的：

“亲爱的朋友们：

“我不打算以女士们和先生们称呼你们，因为，我太了解你们了。”

(44)

An American tourist in France found that he had a two hours´ wait for his train at a junction, and set out to explore the neighborhood. He discovered at last that he was lost, and could not find his way back to the station. He therefore addressed a passer-by in the best French he could recollect from his college days, mispronouncing it with great emphasis. He voiced his request for information as follows:

"Pardonnez-moi. J´ai quitté ma train et maintenant je ne sais pas où le trouver encore. Est-ce que vous pouvez me montrer le route à la train?"

"Let´s look for it together," said the stranger genially. "I don´t speak French, either."

一位在法国旅游的美国人，等火车的时候，他发现还有两个小时的空闲时间，于是就出发去周围看看。可是，最后他发现自己迷路了，无法找到回火车站的路。于是，他用他能够记得的大学时候学到的仅有的几句法语向一个过路人问路，他的重音错误百出，不过还是这样讲出了自己的问题：

“对不起。我离开了我的火车，现在不知道怎么找到它。您能给我指到火车的路线吗？”

“我们一起找吧，”过路人温和地说。“我也不会说法语。”

(45)

There was a haunted house down South which was carefully avoided by all the superstitious negroes. But a new arrival in the community, named Sam, bragged of his bravery as too superior to be shaken by any ghosts, and declared that, for the small sum of two dollars cash in hand paid, he would pass the night alone in the haunted house. A score of other darkies contributed, and the required amount was raised. It was not, however, to be delivered to the courageous Sam until his reappearance after the vigil. With this understanding the boaster betook himself to the haunted house for the night.

When a select committee sought for Sam next morning, no trace of him was found. Careful search for three days failed to discover the missing negro.

But on the fourth day Sam entered the village street, covered with mud and evidently worn with fatigue.

"Hi, dear, nigger!" one of the bystanders shouted. "What you-all been in the last four days?"

And Sam answered simply:

"I have been coming back."

南方有一个房子闹鬼，附近迷信的黑人都不敢靠近。有一个新来乍到名叫汤姆的黑人，却自夸自己的胆量过人，不怕鬼。他说，只要给他两美元现金，他能在那所闹鬼的房子里单独过夜。其他黑人都纷纷解囊，很快就凑齐了两美元。但是，他们说，要等勇敢的汤姆从鬼屋出来之后，才可以把钱给他。汤姆表示同意，于是，就独自一人前往鬼屋过夜。

第二天，大家派人去找汤姆，却连汤姆的影子也看不见。仔细寻找了三天，也没有发现失踪的汤姆。

到了第四天，汤姆出现在村里的街上，浑身是泥，疲惫不堪。

“喂，亲爱的汤姆！”一个看热闹的人喊道，“这几天你到哪里去了？”

汤姆只回答了一句。

“我一直在往回走。”

（46）

The good wife apologized to her unexpected guests for serving the apple pie without cheese. The little boy of the family slipped quietly away from the table for a moment, and returned with a cube of cheese, which he laid on the guest´s plate. The visitor smiled in recognition of the lad´s thoughtfulness, popped the cheese into his mouth, and then remarked:

"You must have sharper eyes than your

mother, sonny. Where did you find it?"

The boy replied with a flush of pride:

"In the rat–trap."

客人突然来访，女主人端上来苹果派，并且道歉说没有奶酪了。她家的小儿子悄悄地从桌旁溜了出去，过了一会儿，他手里拿着一块奶酪回来了。他把奶酪放在客人的盘子里。客人看到孩子这样周到，欣慰地笑了，他一边把奶酪往嘴里塞，一边说：

"宝贝儿，你的眼睛比你妈妈的还尖。你是在哪里找到奶酪的？"

小男孩骄傲得满脸通红：

"在老鼠夹子里。"

(47)

The young wife greeted her husband tearfully on his return from the day's work.

"Oh, Willie, darling," she gasped, "I have been so insulted!"

"Insulted!" Willie exclaimed wrathfully. "Insulted by whom?"

"By your mother!" the wife declared, and sobbed aloud.

The husband was aghast, but inclined to

be skeptical.

"By my mother, Ella? Why, dearest, that´s nonsense. She´s a hundred miles away."

"But she did," the wife insisted. "A letter came to you this morning, and it was addressed in your mother´s writing, so, of course, I opened it."

"Oh, yes, of course," Willie agreed, without any enthusiasm.

"And it was written to you all the whole way through, every word of it, except—"

"Except what?"

"Except the postscript," the wife flared. "That was the insult—that was to me." The tears flowed again. "It said: ´P. S.—Dear Ella, don´t fail to give this letter to Willie. I want him to read it.´"

丈夫威利下班了，年轻的妻子埃拉满眼是泪地前来相迎。

她泣不成声地说："威利，亲爱的，这简直是侮辱人！"

"侮辱！"威利愤怒地喊道，"谁侮辱你了？"

"你妈妈！"妻子告诉他，大声抽泣着。

丈夫吓了一跳，可是，还是半信半疑。

"你说我妈妈？这不可能，亲爱的，肯定是胡说。她离这儿有一百里呢。"

"可是，就是她。"妻子坚持道，"今天早晨我收到一封信，是你妈妈的笔迹，所以，我就理所当然地拆开看了。"

“那当然，”威利不以为然地点着头。

“信从头到尾每一句话都是写给你的，只有——”

“只有什么？”

“只有附言是给我的，” 妻子愤愤不平地叫道，眼泪又一次流了下来。“这简直是侮辱。附言说：亲爱的埃拉，请务必将此信交给威利。我想让他亲自读。”

（48）

The class had been told by the teacher to write compositions in which they must not attempt any flights of fancy, but should only state what was really in them. The star production from this command was a composition written by a boy who was both sincere and painstaking. It ran as follows:

“I shall not attempt any flights of fancy, but write just what is really in me. In me there is my stomach, lungs, liver, two apples, two cakes and my dinner.”

老师给全班布置了作文，要求只能写他们自身的事情，不能凭空想象。结果，有一篇作文堪称唯命是从的经典之作，该作文出自一个极其认真努力的男孩儿之手。原文是这样的：

“我绝不凭空想象，保证只写我自身的事情。在我身上，有胃、有肺、有肝、有两个苹果、两个蛋糕，还有我的晚饭。”

（49）

The new reporter wrote his concluding paragraph concerning the murder as follows:

“Fortunately for the deceased, he had deposited all of his money in the bank the day before. He lost practically nothing but his life.”

新记者对谋杀案的报道是这样结束的：所幸的是，死者前一天已经将所有的钱都存进了银行。因此，他只丢了性命，别的一无所失。

（50）

Deacon Gibbs explained why he had at last decided to move into town in spite of the fact that he had always declared himself a lover of life in the country. But his explanation was clear and conclusive.

"My third wife, Mirandy, she doesn´t like the country, and what Mirandy she does not like, I just naturally have to hate."

迪肯·吉布斯虽然总是说自己喜欢乡村生活，但是，最终却决定搬到镇上去住。他的解释清楚明确：

"我的第三个老婆梅兰蒂不喜欢乡村，所以，只要是她不喜欢的，我当然就得讨厌。"

(51)

The very youthful son of a henpecked father was in a gloomy mood, rebellious against the conditions of his life. He announced a desperate purpose:

"I´m going to get married. I´m bossed by pa an ma, an´ teacher, an´ I ain´t going to stan´ for it. I´m going to get married right smack off. A married man ain´t bossed by nobody ´cept his wife."

一个妻管严男人的儿子心情沮丧，对自己的生活极其不满。他这样宣布他的迫切愿望：

"我要结婚。在家我受爸爸妈妈的管，在学校受老师的管，我已经忍无可忍了。我想立刻就结婚。因为一个结了婚的男人只受老婆一个人的管。"

(52)

The new clergyman was coming to call, and the mother gave Emma some instructions:

"If he asks your name, say Emma Jane; if he asks how old you are, say you are eight years old; if he asks who made you, say God made me."

It is a fact that the clergyman did ask just those three questions in that order, to the first two of which Emma replied correctly. But it is also a fact that when the minister propounded the third query, as to her origin, the child hesitated, and then said:

"Mama did tell me the man´s name, but I´ve gone and forgotten it."

新来的牧师来家拜访，妈妈叮嘱小艾玛说：

"如果他问你叫什么名字，你就说叫艾玛·简；如果他问你多大了，你就说八岁了；如果他问你是谁创造的你，你就说上帝创造了我。"

果真，牧师问了这几个问题，而且顺序都一样。对于前两个问题，艾玛都回答自如。可是，当牧师问到第三个问题，是谁创造了她时，孩子犹豫了一下，然后说：

"妈妈刚才告诉我那个男人的名字了，但是我忘了。"

(53)

The disreputable-looking panhandler picked out an elderly gentleman of most benevolent aspect and made a plea for a small financial contribution. When he had finished his narrative of misery and woe the elderly gentleman replied benignantly:

"My good friend, I have no money, but I can give you some good advice."

The tramp spat contemptuously, and uttered an oath of disgust.

"If you have got no money," he jeered, "I reckon your advice isn't worth hearing."

一个衣衫褴褛的乞丐，走到一位面善的老绅士面前，求他发发慈悲给点儿钱。当他陈述完自己的不幸遭遇和悲惨境地之后，老先生温和地说：

"我的好朋友，我没钱，可是我可以给你一些忠告。"

这个乞丐立刻轻蔑地朝地上啐了一口，不屑地咒骂道：

"如果你没钱，那你的忠告也就不值一听了。"

(54)

The new clergyman in the country parish, during his visit to an old lady of his flock, inquired if she accepted the doctrine of Falling from Grace. The good woman nodded vigorously.

"Yes, sir," she declared with pious zeal, "I believe in it, and, praise the Lord! I practice it!"

村里新来了一个牧师。有一次，他去拜访教区里一位老妇人，他问她是否接受人类堕落之说。虔诚的女人不断地点头。

"是的，先生，"她满怀虔诚地说，"我不但接受，而且，感谢主！我也身体力行！"

(55)

"And you say you have the same nightmare every night," the doctor inquired. "What is it?"

The suffering man answered:

"I dream that I´m married."

"Ah, hum!" the physician grunted perfunctorily. "To whom?"

"To my wife," the patient explained. "That´s what makes it a nightmare."

医生问："你说你每天晚上都做同一个噩梦？你梦到什么了？"

饱受噩梦折磨的男人回答：

"我梦见我结婚了。"

"啊，嗯。" 医生不置可否地随意问道："和谁？"

"和我妻子，"病人解释。"所以，太可怕了。"

(56)

The mourning widow caused a tender sentiment to be chiseled on the headstone of her husband´s grave. The exact wording was as follows:

"Thou are at rest, until we meet again."

刚刚丧夫的寡妇让人在丈夫的墓碑上刻下了温情脉脉的词句。具体内容如下：

"趁我还没来，你先安息吧！"

(57)

The indignant householder held up before the policeman the dead cat that had been lying by the curb three days.

"What am I to do with this?" he demanded.

"Take it to headquarters," was the serene reply. "If nobody claims it within a reasonable time, it´s your property."

愤怒的房主拿起那只已经在路边躺了三天的死猫给警察看。

"我该拿它怎么办？"他问。

"把它带到总部去，"警察平静地回答。"如果在规定期限内，无人认领，它就属于你了。"

(58)

The young man, who was notorious for the reckless driving of his car, was at his home in the country, when he received a telephone call, and a woman´s voice asked if he intended to go motoring that afternoon.

"No, not this afternoon," he replied. "But why do you ask? Who are you?"

"That doesn´t matter," came the voice over the wire. "It´s only that I wish to send my little girl down the street on an errand."

有一个年轻人，开车横冲直撞出了名。有一天，在乡间的家里，他接到一个电话，一个女人问下午他是否打算出去飙车。

"不，今天下午不去，"年轻人回答。"可是，你为什么要问这个？你是谁？"

"这个无关紧要，"电话线那边的声音说。"我只是打算让我的小女儿到街上去买点儿东西。"

(59)

The Sunday-school teacher examined his new class.

"Who made the world?" he demanded. Nobody seemed to know. He repeated the question somewhat sternly. As the silence persisted, he frowned and spoke with increased severity:

"Children, I must know who made the world!"

Then, at last, a small boy piped up in much agitation:

"Oh, sir, please, sir, it wasn't me!"

星期日学校里，老师问他新带的班：

"谁创造了这个世界？"好像没人知道。他又很严肃地重复了一遍这个问题。还是沉默，他皱起了眉头，语气更加严肃地说：

“孩子们，你们必须告诉我是谁创造了这个世界！”

最后，一个小男孩局促不安地站了起来：

“噢，先生，求您了，不是我！”

（60）

The fair penitent explained to the confessor how greatly she was grieved by an accusing conscience. She bewailed the fact that she was sadly given over to personal vanity. She added that on this very morning she had gazed into her mirror and had yielded to the temptation of thinking herself beautiful.

“Is that all, my daughter?” the priest demanded.

“Then, my daughter,” the confessor bade her, “go in peace, for to be mistaken is not to sin.”

一个女士对神父忏悔说，她因受到良心的谴责而非常痛苦。她承认自己图慕虚荣，因为当天早晨，她照镜子的时候，竟然屈从于内心的诱惑，认为自己很美丽。

“就这些吗？我的孩子？”神父问道，“那么，我的孩子，”神父安慰她说，“安心去吧，因为错误的想法不是罪恶。”

(61)

The Professor: A diamond is the hardest known substance, in as much as it will cut glass.

The Cynic: Glass! My dear sir, a diamond will even make an impression on a woman´s heart.

教授：钻石是最坚硬的物质，因为可以用它来割玻璃。

好挖苦人的人：岂止割玻璃！我亲爱的先生，钻石甚至可以在女人的心上留下印痕。

(62)

A man and his eldest son went to have their photographs taken together, and the photographer said to the young man, “It will make a better picture if you put your hand on your father´s shoulder.”

"H'm," said the father, "it would make a more natural picture if he put it in my pocket."

一个男人和他的长子照合影。摄影师对年轻人说，"如果你把手放在你父亲的肩膀上，照片会显得自然些。"

"噢，" 父亲说，"如果他把手放在我的口袋里，照片会更加自然。"

(63)

"Miss Smith–Belinda," sighed the young man, passionately, "there is something I want to tell you–something that I——"

"What is it?" asked the girl, as she leaned back in her chair, with a bored expression on her face.

The young man drew a long breath, and his face turned to dull purple. "It is a question which is very near to any heart," he said awkwardly. "Could you–do you think you could ever marry a man like me?"

"Oh, yes," replied Belinda, quite calmly, "that is, if he wasn't too much like you!"

"史密斯小姐——贝琳达，" 年轻人喘了口气，热切地说，"我想告诉你一件事情——一件我——"

"什么事？"女孩向椅子靠去，面露倦意。

年轻人长长地吸了一口气，脸涨得发紫。"是我发自内心的一个问题，"他尴尬地说。"你会，你觉得你会嫁给像我这样的人吗？"

"噢，当然，"贝琳达回答，语气很平静，"只要他不是太像你。"

(64)

The maiden of, er-forty or so, was much upset.

Quote she to a younger friend:

"Kate talks so outrageously. Yesterday she actually told me I was nothing but a hopeless old maid."

"That´s pretty frank!" exclaimed the friend.

"Yes,wasn´t it unladylike of her?"

"It certainly was rude," agreed the other. "Still, it´s better than having her tell lies about you."

一位年约 40 岁的老姑娘，很不开心。

她对稍微年少一点的闺中密友说：

"凯特说话太可恶了。昨天，她竟然说我只不过是个毫无希望的老处女。"

“她这话说得太过直率！”朋友说。

“是的，可是，她是不是不够淑女？”

“没错，她说话是有些粗鲁，”朋友附和道，“不过，她说的也还是实话。”

(65)

“He proposed to me last night, mother. What shall I do?”

“But, my dear daughter, you've only known him three weeks.”

“I know that, mother, but on the other hand if I delay in accepting him he might find out some things about me he won't like, too.”

“妈妈，他昨晚向我求婚了。我该怎么办？”

“可是，我亲爱的女儿，你认识他才三个星期。”

“我知道，可是，妈妈，话说回来，如果我现在不答应他，他以后一样有可能发现我的缺点。”

(66)

She (tenderly): "And are mine the only lips you have kissed?"

He: "Yes, and they are the sweetest of all."

她(温柔地):"你只亲吻过我的嘴唇吗?"

他:"是的,所有嘴唇里面,你的最香甜。"

(67)

Papa: "Why did you permit young Gay bird to kiss you in the parlor last night?"

Daughter: "Because I was afraid he´d catch cold in the hall."

爸爸:"昨晚,你为什么允许那个家伙在客厅里亲你?"

女儿:"因为我担心在走廊里他会感冒。"

(68)

Interviewer: "What sort of girls make the best show-girls?"

Stage Manager: "Those who have the most to show, of course."

考官："什么样的女孩儿能成为最佳秀女？"

舞台经理："当然是那些最有东西可秀的女孩儿。"

（69）

On Johnnie's return from the birthday party, his mother expressed the hope that he had behaved politely at the luncheon table, and properly said, "Yes, if you please" and "No, thank you," when anything was offered him.

Johnnie shook his head seriously.

"I guess I didn't say, 'No, thank you.' I ate everything there was."

约翰参加完生日晚会回到家，妈妈问他在餐桌上的表现是否得体，在主人邀请他吃东西的时候,他说没说"好的,请吧"或者"不用了,谢谢。"

约翰很认真地摇了摇头。

"我好像没说'不用了,谢谢。'因为,所有的东西,都被我吃了。"

(70)

As the boat was sinking, the skipper lifted his voice to ask:

"Does anybody know how to pray?"

One man spoke confidently in answer:

"Yes, Captain, I do."

The captain nodded.

"That's all right then," he declared. "You go ahead and pray. The rest of us will put on life-belts. They're one short."

船要沉了,船长高声问道:

"谁会祈祷?"

一个男人自信地回答:

"我会,船长。"

船长点点头。

"这回好了,"他宣布。"现在你祈祷,其他人穿上救生衣。刚好少一个救生衣。"

(71)

First Voter: "So Mr. Jones has been elected. You voted for him, of course?"

Second Voter: "No, I voted for the other man. You see, Mr. Jones supported Woman's Suffrage, which I abhor."

投票人 1:“琼斯先生当选了。你肯定投他的票了,对吗?”

投票人 2:“没有,我投了别人的票。你知道,琼斯先生支持妇女拥有选举权,而我对此深恶痛绝。”

(72)

She: “Oh! Jack! Are you perfectly certain that you love me?”

He: “My darling! You don´t suppose that I have lived for thirty years without knowing love when I feel it.”

她:“噢! 杰克! 你肯定你真的爱我吗?”

他:“亲爱的! 我都三十岁了,你该不会以为我还不知道爱情的滋味吧?”

(73)

Best Man (seeing couple off on honeymoon): “Here you are—just a few magazines to help pass away the time.”

男傧相(送新婚夫妇去度蜜月):“给——这有几份杂志,拿着消磨时间吧。”

(74)

Mr. Househunter: “I don´t care for those flats we looked at to-day. The rooms are too narrow, and the ceilings are too low.”

Mrs. Househunter: “But they are cheap, dear; and you and I are neither very wide nor very high.”

寻房先生：“我觉得今天看的这些公寓都不怎么样。房间太窄，房顶太低。”

寻房夫人：“可是亲爱的，这些房子便宜，再说，我们都不宽，也不高。”

(75)

The woman wrote a reference for her discharged cook as follows:

“Maggie Flynn has been employed by me for a month. She is an excellent cook, but I could not afford to make use of her services longer.”

The husband, who was present, afterward expressed his surprise at the final clause.

“But it´s true,” the wife answered. “The dishes she smashed cost double her wages.”

一位家庭主妇在解雇她家的厨师时，为他写了这样的评语：

“麦琪·弗林在我这里工作了一月。她是个非常出色的厨师，但是，我已经雇不起她了。”

她的丈夫刚好在一旁，看了她写的后半句话，表示不能理解。

主妇辩解道：“事实的确如此，她打碎的盘子是她工资的两倍。”

(76)

“Oh! Are you really a mind-reader?”

“Yes! I am.”

“Then I hope you aren´t offended. I didn´t mean what I thought about you.”

“哇！你真的可以看透别人的心思吗？”

“当然了。”

“那么希望你不要介意我对你的看法。我不是故意的。”

(77)

“I want to buy you something useful for your birthday. What can you suggest?”

“Oh! I think a really useful diamond ring

would do as well as anything."

"我打算给你买一个比较实用的生日礼物。你有什么建议吗?"

"哦,那么就钻戒吧,它比什么都实用。"

(78)

Prospective Bride: "I am glad I decided to be married in a traveling dress–a wedding dress costs such a lot."

Dressmaker: "Yes, miss, and the next time you wanted to wear it, it would be out of fashion."

有远见的新娘:"很高兴我打算穿旅行服结婚——结婚礼服太贵了。"

裁缝:"没错,小姐,可下次你再想穿它的时候,它就已经过时了。"

(79)

Man: "Yes, the doctors saved my life, but it cost me over a thousand dollars."

Woman: "Oh! what extravagance!"

男士:"没错,医生救了我的命,花了我一千多美元。"

女士:"哇!你太奢侈了!"

(80)

Jones (who is of an inquiring mind): "Aren't you getting tired of hearing people say, 'That is the beautiful Miss Belsize!'?"

Miss Bel (a professional beauty): "Oh, no. I'm getting tired of hearing people say, 'Is that the beautiful Miss Belsize?'"

琼斯（一个好奇心很强的人）："总是听大家说'那就是漂亮的贝尔小姐！'你不觉得烦吗？"

贝尔小姐（一个大众美女）："哦，不烦。我烦的是有人问'那位是不是漂亮的贝尔小姐？'"

(81)

She: "No! I can't give you another dance. But I'll introduce you to the prettiest girl in the room!"

He: "But I don't want to dance with the prettiest girl in the room. I want to dance with you!"

她："对不起，我不能跟你跳下一支舞。不过，我可以介绍这里最漂亮的女孩儿给你。"

他："可是，我不想跟这里最漂亮的女孩儿跳舞，我想跟你跳舞。"

(82)

Sympathetic Lady: What´s the matter with your hand, my little man?

Boy: Sawed the top of my finger off.

Sympathetic Lady: Dear, dear, how did you do that?

Boy: Sawing.

好心的女士:你的手怎么了,孩子?

男孩:我的手指尖被锯掉了。

好心的女士:哦,天哪,你怎么弄的?

男孩:锯的。

(83)

It was a case of attempted murder, in which the prisoner was accused of having fired twice at his intended victim. One of the witnesses for the prosecution was being severely cross-examined by the defending counsel.

"You say that you heard both shots fired?" he asked sternly.

"Yes, sir."

"How near were you to the scene of the affair?"

"At the time the first shot was fired I

was about twenty feet from the prisoner."

"Twenty feet. Humph! Now tell the court how far you were off when you heard the second shot."

"Well, sir," replied the witness slowly, "I didn´t exactly measure the distance; but, speaking approximately, I should say about half a mile."

这是一个谋杀未遂的案件，罪犯被控两次向被害人开枪。辩护律师对其中的一名目击证人进行了严格盘问。

"你说你听到了两声枪响？"他严厉地问道。

"是的，先生。"

"案发时你距离现场有多远？"

"第一次枪响时我距离罪犯大约二十英尺。"

"二十英尺。那么请你告诉法庭，听到第二次枪声时你距离罪犯有多远。"

"呃，先生，" 证人慢条斯理地说，"具体多少，我没有量过。不过，估计有半英里。"

(84)

Sandy had gone to the station to see his cousin off.

"Mac," he said, "you like to leave me a

bob or two to drink you a safe journey."

"I cannot," was the reply. "And my spare cash I give to my old mother."

"That's strange! Your mother said you never gave her anything!"

"Well, if I don't give my old mother anything, what sort of chance do you think you've got?"

桑迪去火车站送他的堂弟。

他说："麦克，你能不能给我一先令或者两先令，我想为你的平安到达喝两杯。"

麦克回答："不行，剩下的钱我要都给我老妈。"

"那太奇怪了！你妈妈说你从来什么都不给她。"

"所以，如果我连我老妈都什么也不给，你想你还有希望从我这里得到什么吗？"

(85)

Pompous Publisher (to aspiring novice in literature): I have been reading your manuscript, my dear lady, and there is much in it. I think—ahem!—very good. But there are parts somewhat vague. Now, you should always write so that the most ignorant can understand.

Youthful Authoress (wishing to show herself

most ready to accept advice): Oh, yes, I´m sure. But, tell me, which are the parts that have given you trouble?

自负的出版人（对热情洋溢的文学新秀）：亲爱的女士，我一直在读你的稿子，我认为你的作品很有思想——啊咳——很好。可是，有一些地方有点含糊不清。这样说吧，你写的东西应该让哪怕最无知的人也能看明白。

年轻的女作者（急切地想表白她是多么愿意接受建议）：哦，好的，我明白了。那您能不能告诉我哪些地方让您费神了？

（86）

Professor (endeavoring to impress on class the definition of cynic): Young man, what would you call a man who pretends to know everything?

Senior: A professor!

教授（试图让全班同学深刻体会什么是愤世嫉俗的人）：年轻人，你们怎么称呼一个假装什么都懂的人？

大四的学生：我们叫他教授！

(87)

Sister: "Hubby received an anonymous letter this morning informing him of something I did before we were married."

Brother: "Well, the best thing you can do is to confess."

Sister: "I know it, but he won´t let me read the letter and I don´t know what to confess."

妹妹:"我丈夫今天早晨收到一封匿名信,是有关我结婚前的事情的。"

哥哥:"你最好如实坦白。"

妹妹:"我明白,可是他不让我看信,所以我也不知道该坦白什么。"

(88)

After years of endeavor in poverty, the inventor made a success, and came running home with pockets bulging real money. He joyously strewed thousand-dollar bills in his wife´s lap, crying:

"Now, at last, my dear, you will be able to buy you some decent clothes."

"I´ll do nothing of the kind," was the sharp retort. "I´ll get the same kind the other women are wearing."

在贫困中挣扎了许多年的发明家，终于取得了成功。他口袋里装满了钞票，兴冲冲地跑回家，把千元一张的钞票堆放在妻子的腿上，喊道："亲爱的，现在你终于可以买几件体面的衣服了。"

"我可不想买什么体面的衣服，"妻子厉声反驳道，"我只想买和别的女人身上穿的一样的衣服。"

(89)

Young Woman (holding out hand): Will you please tell me how to pronounce the name of the stone in this ring? Is it turquoise?

Jeweler (after inspecting it): The correct pronunciation is "glass."

青年女子(伸出手):您能告诉我这个戒指上这颗宝石的名字怎么念吗?是念"绿宝石"吗?

珠宝商（看了看宝石）：正确的读法应该是"玻璃"。

(90)

"I took that pretty girl from the store home the other night, and stole a kiss."

"What did she say?"

"Will that be all?"

"那天晚上我把商店的那个漂亮女孩儿带回家,趁她不注意亲了她一下。"

"她怎么说?"

"这就完了?"

3. 童言无忌

Kids Say It All

(91)

A little girl four years old was alone in the nursery with the door closed and fastened when her little brother arrived and expressed a desire to come in. The following was the dialogue:

"I wants to tum in, Sissy."

"But you tan't tum in, Tom."

"But I wants to."

"Well, I'm in my nightie gown an' nurse says little boys mus'n't see little girls in their nightie gowns."

There was a period of silence during which the astonished little boy reflected on the mystery. It was ended by Sissy's calling out:

"You tan tum in now, Tom—I tooked it off."

托儿所里，一个四岁的小女孩儿独自一人待在房间里，房门紧闭。这时，她的小弟弟来了，想进屋。下面是他们的对话：

“姐姐，我想进去。”

“汤姆，你不能进来。”

“可是，我想进去。”

“我穿着睡衣呢，阿姨说小女孩儿穿睡衣的时候，不许小男孩儿看见。”

小男孩懵了，想不明白这到底是怎么回事。正在他不知所措的时候，姐姐说话了：

“汤姆，现在你可以进来了——我把睡衣脱掉了。”

(92)

The tiny boy fell down and bumped his head. His Uncle Bill picked the child up, with the remark:

“Now I´ll kiss it, and the pain will all be gone.”

The youngster recovered his smiles under the treatment, and then, as he was set down, addressed his uncle eagerly:

“Come down in the kitchen—the cook has the toothache.”

小男孩儿摔倒了，头上碰了个包。舅舅比尔一边抱起孩子一边说：

“让我来亲亲你的头，这样就不疼了。”

果然，小男孩儿被亲吻后脸上又露出了笑容。

随后，他脚一落地便急切地对舅舅说：

“快去厨房——厨娘的牙疼。”

（93）

Jeanette was wearing a new frock when her dearest friend called.

“I look a perfect fright,” she remarked, eager for praise.

The dearest friend was thinking of her own affairs, and answered absent-mindedly:

“Yes, you certainly do.”

“Oh, you horrid thing!” Jeanette gasped. “I'll never—never speak to you again!”

珍妮刚穿上一件新衣服，她最好的朋友来了。

“我看起来一定很难看吧，”她嘴上这么说，可是心里却期待着朋友的赞赏。

刚巧，她的好朋友正想着自己的心事，随口就答了一句，“是的，难看死了。”

“噢，你真讨厌！”珍妮气急了。“我再也……再也不跟你说话了！”

(94)

The small boy sat at the foot of a telegraph pole, with a tin can in his hands. The curious old gentleman gazed first at the lad and then at the can, much perplexed.

"Caterpillars! What are you doing with them?"

"They climb trees and eat the leaves," the boy explained.

"Yes? "

"And so," the boy continued proudly, "I´m fooling this bunch by letting them climb the telegraph pole."

一个小男孩儿坐在电线杆下，手里拿着一个锡罐儿。一位老人好奇地看了看男孩儿，又看了看锡罐，非常不解地问：

"毛毛虫！你拿它们做什么？"

"它们爬树，吃树叶，"男孩儿解释说。

"那又怎样？"

"所以，"男孩儿得意地回答，"我就骗它们来爬这个电线杆。"

(95)

"Come, Dorothy," said her father impatiently, "throw your doll on the bed and hurry or we shall be late."

"Daddy, how can you?" reproved the child. "I isn´t´ that kind of a mother."

"快点儿，桃乐茜，"爸爸不耐烦地说，"把你的玩具娃娃扔到床上，快走，要不我们就迟到了。"

"爸爸，你怎么能这样说？"孩子责备道，"我可不是那种妈妈。"

(96)

Mother: "Oh, Mary, why do you wipe your mouth with the back of your hand?"

Mary: "´Because it´s so much cleaner than the front."

妈妈："喂，玛丽，你为什么要用手背擦嘴？"

玛丽："因为手背比手心干净。"

(97)

"Mamma!"

"What is it, dear?"

"It seems to me that a silly question is

something that you don´t know the answer to."

"妈妈!"

"怎么了,孩子?"

"我发现愚蠢的问题就是您答不上来的问题。"

(98)

The teacher put a question to the class:

"What does a cat have that no other animal has?"

A number cried in unison:

"Fur!"

But an objector raised the point that bears and skunks have fur. One pupil raised an eager hand:

"I know, teacher—whiskers!"

But another objector laughed scornfully.

"Haw-haw! My papa has whiskers!"

The suggester of whiskers defended her idea by declaring: "My papa hasn´t got whiskers."

"Because he can´t!" the objector sneered. "Haw-haw! Your pa is no good. My pa says—"

The teacher rapped for order, and repeated her question. A little girl raised her hand, and at the teacher's nod spoke timidly.

"Kittens!"

老师问全班：

"什么东西猫有，可是别的动物却没有？"

几个学生异口同声地大声回答道：

"毛皮！"

一个同学反对说，熊和臭鼬也有毛皮。另一个同学迫不及待地举起了手：

"老师，我知道——是胡子！"

另一个同学不屑一顾地说：

"哈哈，我爸爸也有胡子！"

回答"胡子"的同学反驳道："我爸爸就没有胡子。"

"那是因为他长不了胡子！" 那位同学讥讽道，"哈哈，你爸爸不怎么样嘛，我爸说……"

老师敲着桌子让大家安静，然后又重复了一遍问题。这时，一个小女孩儿举起了手，在老师的点头鼓励下，怯生生地说：

"是猫咪宝宝！"

(99)

The little girl returned from church deeply musing on the sermon, in which the preacher had declared that animals, lacking souls, could not go to heaven. As the result of her meditation, she presented a problem to the family at the dinner table, when she asked earnestly:

"If cats don´t go to heaven, where do the angels get the strings for their harps?"

小女孩从教堂出来，一路上都在想刚才布道中教士说过的话：动物没有灵魂，所以不能上天堂。回到家，小女孩在餐桌上非常认真地问："如果猫不去天堂，那么天使们拿什么做竖琴上的琴弦呢？"

（注：据说，猫的肠线<cat gut>是做竖琴琴弦的原料。）

(100)

The mother catechised her young son just before the hour for the arrival of the music teacher.

"Have you washed your hands very carefully?"

"Yes, mother."

"And have you washed your face thoroughly?"

"Yes, mother."

"And were you particular to wash behind your ears?"

"On her side I did, mother."

还有一个小时音乐老师就要来了，妈妈问年幼的儿子：

"你的手洗干净了吗？"

"洗了，妈妈。"

"你的脸洗干净了吗？"

"洗了，妈妈。"

"耳朵背后，你很仔细地洗过了吗？"

"靠老师那边的洗了，妈妈。"

(101)

Jimmy found much to criticize in his small sister. He felt forced to remonstrate with his mother.

"Don't you want Jenny to be a good wife like you when she grows up?" he demanded. His mother nodded assent.

"Then you better get busy, ma. You make me give into her all the time 'cause I'm bigger 'en she is. You're smaller 'en pa, but when he comes in, you bring him his slippers, and hand him the paper." Jimmie yanked his go-cart from baby Jennie, and disregarded her wail of anger as he continued:

"Got to discipline her, or she´ll make an awful wife!"

小吉姆觉得他的小妹妹有很多毛病，所以他感到有必要和妈妈谈谈。

“您不是打算让珍妮长大后像您一样当个好妻子吗？”他问。母亲点头表示赞同。

“妈，那您最好赶快做点儿什么。无论什么事情您都让我让着她，因为她比我小。可是，您不是也比爸爸小吗？为什么爸爸一回来，您就给他拿拖鞋，递报纸呢？”小吉姆说着说着一下子就将他的玩具车从小珍妮那里拽了过来。小珍妮生气地大哭起来，可是吉姆毫不理会，他继续对妈妈说：

“得教训她，要不，她会变成一个糟糕的妻子的。”

(102)

The young clergyman during a parochial call noticed that the little daughter of the hostess was busy with her slate while eying him closely from time to time.

"And what are you doing, Clara?" he asked, with his most engaging smile.

"I´m drawing a picture of you," was the

answer.

The clerical visitor sat very still to facilitate the work of the artist. But, presently, Clara shook her head in discouragement.

"I don´t like it much," she confessed. "I guess I´ll put a tail on it, and call it a dog."

一位年轻的牧师去教区的一户人家巡访。他发现主人家的小女儿正在书写板上描画着什么，而且还不时地打量他。

牧师笑眯眯地问："克拉拉，你在干什么呀？"

"我在给你画像。"小女孩儿回答。

于是，年轻的牧师保持坐姿，让小艺术家好画些。可是，很快，克拉拉灰心丧气地摇起了头，"画得不好，"她坦言道，"我想我还是添个尾巴，画成一条狗算了。"

(103)

The group of dwellers at the seaside was discussing the subject of dreams and their significance. During a pause, one of the party turned to a little girl who had sat listening intently, and asked:

"Do you believe that dreams come true?"

"Of course, they do," the child replied firmly. "Last night I dreamed that I went paddling—and I had!"

有一群人在海边宿营。他们讨论着梦想和梦想的意义。讨论间歇中，一个人转向坐在一旁认真听讲的一个小女孩儿，问道：

"你相信梦想会成真吗？"

"当然会成真了。"女孩儿肯定地回答。"昨天晚上我梦见我玩水了，我真的玩水了。"

（注：此处的幽默在于小女孩将抽象的梦想当成了具体的梦境。）

（104）

The little boy was found by his mother with pencil and paper, making a sketch. When asked what he was doing, he answered promptly, and with considerable pride:

"I'm drawing a picture of God."

"But," gasped the shocked mother, "you cannot do that. No one has seen God. No one knows how God looks."

"Well," the little boy replied, complacently, "when I get through they will."

妈妈发现小男孩儿手里拿着铅笔和纸，正在勾画着什么。妈妈问他在画什么，他立刻不无骄傲地回答：

“我在画上帝。”

“可是，”妈妈惊恐地倒吸了口气，“你不能那样做。谁也没有见过上帝。谁也不知道上帝长得什么样。”

“没关系，” 小男孩儿沾沾自喜地回答说，等我画完了，他们就知道了。

(105)

The boy hurried home to his father with an announcement:

"Me and Joe Peck had a fight to-day."

The father nodded gravely.

"Mr. Peck has already called to see me about it."

The little boy's face brightened.

"Gee, pop! I hope you made out as well as I did!"

男孩儿匆匆跑回家，向父亲宣布了一个消息：

“今天我和乔·派克打了一架。”

爸爸沉重地点了点头：

“派克的爸爸已经打来电话说要来找我解决这件事。”

小男孩儿的脸上露出兴奋的神情。

“太棒了，爸爸！希望你和我一样能打赢！”

(106)

The kindly lady accosted the little boy on the beach, who stood with downcast head, and grinding his toes into the sand and looking very miserable and lonely indeed.

"Haven´t you anybody to play with?" she inquired sympathetically.

The boy shook his head forlornly, as he explained:

"I have one friend—but I hate him!"

海滩上，一个男孩儿低着头，用力踢着沙子，他看起来很难过，很孤独。一位好心的女士走向前同情地问道："没有人和你玩吗？"

男孩儿无奈地摇了摇头，解释说：

"我有一个朋友——可是我恨他！"

(107)

This is the dialogue between a little girl and a little boy:

"What are you bawling about, Jimmie?"

"I´m crying because my mum has gone to heaven."

"That´s silly. Maybe she hasn´t."

下面是一个小女孩儿和一个小男孩儿之间的对话：

"吉姆,你哭什么?"

"我哭是因为我妈妈去了天堂。"

"不用哭。也许她没去呢。"

(108)

The mother came on her little son who was standing thoughtfully before the gooseberry bush in the garden. She noted that his expression was both puzzled and distressed.

"Why, what's the matter, little lamb?" she asked tenderly.

"I'm thinking, mum," the boy answered.

"What about, little man?"

"Have gooseberries any legs, mother?"

"Why, no! Of course not, dear."

The perplexity passed from the little boy's face, but the expression of trouble deepened, as he spoke again:

"Then, muvver, I fink I've swallowed a caterpillar."

一个小男孩儿若有所思地站在花园的醋栗丛前,妈妈走过来,发现他表情痛苦迷茫。

"怎么了?小宝贝?"妈妈温柔地问。

"我在想问题,"男孩儿回答。

"我的小男子汉,你想的是什么问题呢?"

"妈妈,醋栗有腿吗?"

"腿？当然没有，亲爱的。"

小男孩儿脸上迷茫的表情消失了，但是，说话的时候，却更加痛苦。

"妈妈，我想刚才我吃的肯定是毛毛虫。"

(109)

The child went with her mother on a visit in New Jersey. At bedtime, the little girl was nervous over the strangeness of her surroundings, but the mother comforted her, saying:

"Remember, dear, God´s angels are all about you."

A little later, a cry from the child called the mother back into the room.

"The angels are buzzing all around just dreadful, mama, and they bite!"

孩子随着妈妈去新泽西旅游。睡觉的时候，面对陌生的环境，她有点儿害怕。妈妈安慰她说：

"记住，亲爱的，上帝的天使就在你周围。"

过了一会儿，孩子叫喊着，又把妈妈召回到她的房间：

"那些天使一个劲地嗡嗡叫，太讨厌了，妈妈，她们还咬人。"

(110)

The son of the house addressed his mother wistfully.

"I´m going to have a little sister some day, ain´t I?"

"Why, dear, do you want one?"

The child nodded seriously.

"Yes, mama, I do. It gets kind of tiresome teasing the cat."

儿子充满渴望地对妈妈说：

"有一天，我会有一个小妹妹吧？"

"嗯，亲爱的，难道你想要一个小妹妹？"

孩子认真地点了点头。

"是的，妈妈，我想要。每天只能欺负小猫，我都烦了。"

(111)

Tiny Clara heard her mother say that a neighboring lady had a new baby. The tot puzzled over the matter, and at last sought additional information:

"Oh, mumsy, what is she going to do with her old one?"

小克拉拉听她妈妈说邻居家的阿姨生了一个新宝宝，这孩子便困惑起来，想了半天，最后说：

“妈妈，阿姨家的那个旧宝宝怎么办？”

(112)

A stranger rang the door-bell. Little eight-year-old Willie Jones opened the door.

“Is Mr. Jones in?” the caller inquired.

Little Willie answered with formal politeness:

“I'm Mr. Jones. Or did you wish to see old Mr. Jones?”

一位陌生人按响了门铃。八岁的小威廉·琼斯去开门。

“琼斯先生在家吗？”来人问。

小威廉很礼貌地回答：

“我就是琼斯先生。莫非您是找老琼斯先生？”

(113)

The kind lady stopped to tell the sobbing little girl not to cry, and she offered as a convincing argument:

“You know it makes little girls homely.”

The child stared belligerently at the benevolent lady, and then remarked:

"You must have cried an awful lot when you was young."

心地善良的女士停下脚步，安慰正在哭泣的小女孩儿不要再哭了，她这样劝解小女孩儿：

"你要知道，眼泪会让小女孩儿变丑的。"

小女孩儿不服气地盯着善良的女士看了一会儿，然后说：

"那您小的时候，肯定流过很多眼泪吧。"

(114)

The little girl evidently appreciated the fact that all men and women are liars, for the following is recorded as the dialogue between her and her mother when she had been caught in a fib:

Mother: "It is very naughty to tell untruths, Kitty. Those who do so, never go to heaven."

Kitty: "Don´t you ever tell an untruth, Mummy?"

Mother: "No, dear, never."

Kitty: "Well, you´ll be fearfully lonely, won´t you, with only George Washington?"

很显然，小女孩儿相信所有的人都撒谎。于是在她的谎言被揭穿之后，就有了她和母亲之间的这段对话：

母亲："基蒂，撒谎很不好。知道吗，撒谎的人永远也去不了天堂。"

基蒂："妈妈，难道你从来没撒过谎吗？"

母亲："从来没有，亲爱的。"

基蒂："噢，那你肯定很孤单，对吧？因为将来只有乔治·华盛顿跟你在一起。"

(115)

Mr. and Mrs. Smith had been invited to a friend's for tea, and the time had arrived for preparing for the visit. "Come along, dearie," said Mr. Smith to her three-year-old son, "and have your face washed."

"Don't want to be washed," came the reply.

"But," said mother, "you don't want to be a dirty boy, do you? I want my little boy to have a nice, clean face for the ladies to kiss."

Upon this persuasion he gave way, and was washed. A few minutes later he stood watching his father washing. "Ha, ha, daddy!" he cried, "I know why you're washing!"

史密斯夫妇受邀去朋友家喝茶，出发前，史密斯夫人对她三岁的儿子说："过来，小宝贝，咱们洗洗脸。"

"不洗，"孩子回答。

"可是，"妈妈说，"你不愿意成为一个脏兮兮的孩子吧？我想让我的小宝贝把脸洗得干干净净，漂漂亮亮的，这样阿姨们就会亲你了。"

听了这样的哄劝，孩子让步了，洗了脸。几分钟之后，他站在那里看他爸爸也在洗脸，于是喊道，"哈，哈，爸爸，我知道你为什么洗脸了！"

（116）

The sister spoke admiringly to the collegian who was calling on her after field day, at which she had been present.

"And how they did applaud when you broke that record!"

Her little brother, who overheard, sniffed indignantly.

"Pa didn´t applaud me for the one I broke," he complained. "He licked me."

一个刚刚参加完比赛的同学来家里做客，姐姐满怀敬仰地对这位同学说：

"你打破纪录的时候，大家的掌声别提有多热烈了！"

弟弟刚好听见这句话，他愤愤不平地说道：

“我打破唱片的时候，老爸可没给我鼓掌，还揍了我一顿。”

(注：英语中，记录和唱片是同一个单词“record”。)

（117）

Elsie: “When is my birthday, Mother?”

Her Mother: “On the thirty-first of this month, dear.”

Elsie: “Oh! Mother! Supposing this month had had only thirty days, where would I have been?”

埃尔希：“妈妈，我生日是什么时候？”

妈妈：“这个月的 31 号。”

埃尔希：“噢！妈妈！假如这个月只有 30 天，我会在哪里呢？”

（118）

Betty: “Mummy, does God send us our food?”

Mother: “Yes, dear; of course He does.”

Betty: “But what a price!”

贝蒂:“妈咪,我们的食物是上帝送来的吗?”

母亲:“是的,亲爱的。”

贝蒂:“哇,太奢侈了!”

(119)

Freddie (aged six): “Mother, you know that lovely purse you gave me for my birthday?”

His Mother: “Yes, dear! What of it?”

Freddie: “It makes me feel awful to think of it just lying in the drawer without a cent in its stomach.”

弗雷迪(六岁):“妈妈,还记得我过生日的时候,您送给我的那个漂亮钱包吗?”

妈妈:“当然记得,小宝贝儿!怎么了?”

弗雷迪:“一想到钱包躺在抽屉里,肚子里没有一分钱,我就很难过。”

(120)

Elsie: “Mummy! if I was a fairy I′d change everything into cake, an′ eat it all up.”

Mother: “I´m afraid such a lot of cake would make you sick.”

Elsie: “Oh! but I´d change myself into an elephant first.”

埃尔希:“妈妈，如果我是仙女我想把所有的东西都变成蛋糕,然后把它吃掉。”

妈妈:“我怕这么多的蛋糕会撑坏你的。”

埃尔希:“噢,不会！我会先把自己变成一头大象。”

(121)

Governess: “Well, Mollie, what are little girls made of?”

Mollie: “Sugar and spice and all that´s nice.”

Governess: “And what are little boys made of?”

Mollie: “Snips and snails and puppy dogs´ tails. I told Bobbie that yesterday, and he could hardly believe it.”

女家庭教师:“茉莉，你知道小女孩儿是用什么做的吗？”

茉莉:“是用糖和香料,还有其他好东西。”

女家庭教师:“那小男孩儿是用什么做的呢？”

茉莉："剪刀、蜗牛和小狗的尾巴。昨天我还告诉博比了，但他不相信。"

(122)

Helen's elder sister: "You know, all the stars are worlds like ours."

Helen: "Well, I shouldn't like to live on one—it would be so horrid when it twinkled."

海伦的姐姐："记住，每颗星星都是一个世界，就像我们的地球一样。"

海伦："但是，我不喜欢待在星星上——它一闪一闪的时候太可怕了。"

(123)

Blinks, after inviting his friend, Jinks, who has just returned from abroad, to dinner, is telling him what a fine memory his little son Bobby has.

"And do you suppose he will remember me?" said Jinks.

"Remember you? Why, he remembers

every face that he ever saw."

An hour later they entered the house, and after Jinks had shaken hands with Mrs. Blinks, he calls Bobby over to him.

"And do you remember me, my little man?"

"Course I do. You're the same man that pa brought home last summer, and ma was so wild about it that she didn't speak to pa for a whole week."

布林科斯邀请刚从国外回来的朋友金克斯吃晚饭,他向朋友夸耀鲍勃超强的记忆力。

"你觉得他还会记得我吗?" 金克斯说。

"你?那当然,只要他见过的脸,他都记得。"

一小时之后,他们到家了,金克斯和布林科斯夫人握过手之后,就把鲍勃叫到身边问:

"还记得我吗,小家伙?"

"当然记得,你就是去年夏天爸爸带回家的那个人,妈妈为此很生气,以至于她一整个礼拜都没跟爸爸说话。"

(124)

Young Harold was late for Sunday-school and the minister inquired the cause. "I was going fishing, but father wouldn't let me," announced the lad.

"That´s the right kind of a father to have," replied the reverend gentleman. "Did he explain the reason why he would not let you go?"

"Yes, sir. He said there wasn´t bait enough for two."

小哈罗德上礼拜课的时候迟到了，牧师问他迟到的原因，他回答："我想去钓鱼，可是爸爸不让。"

德高望重的牧师回答："你有个好爸爸。他告诉你不让你去的原因了吗？"

"是的，先生。他说鱼饵不够两个人用的。"

(125)

The little girl had been naughty in school. By way of punishment, she was directed by the teacher to remain in her seat after the session until she had written an original composition containing not less than fifty words. In a surprisingly short space of time, she offered the following, and was duly excused:

"I lost my kitty, and I went out and called, Come, kitty,

kitty, kitty, kitty, kitty, kitty, kitty, kitty, kitty, kitty, kitty, kitty, kitty, kitty, kitty, kitty, kitty, kitty, kitty."

一个小女孩儿在学校调皮捣蛋，受到惩罚。老师让她下课后待在座位上，写一篇不少于五十字的作文。令人惊奇的是，在很短的时间内，她就完成了任务，得到了宽恕：

“我家的小猫咪丢了，我便出去喊它：“回来，小猫咪，小猫咪，小猫咪，小猫咪，小猫咪，小猫咪，小猫咪，小猫咪，小猫咪，小猫咪，小猫咪，小猫咪。”

(126)

One day a teacher was having a first-grade class in physiology. She asked them if they knew that there was a burning fire in the body all of the time. One little girl spoke up and said:

"Yes´m; when it is a cold day, I can see the smoke."

一天，老师给一年级的学生上生理课。她问学生们是否知道在人的身体里总有一团火在燃烧。一个小女孩儿开口说：

“老师，我知道。天冷的时候，我能看见冒烟。”

(127)

"What are you doing, Marjory?"

"I'm writing a letter to Lily Smif."

"But, darling, you don't know how to write."

"That's no difference, mamma; Lily don't know how to read."

"马克,你在干什么? "

"我在给莉莉写信。"

"可是,亲爱的,你不会写字呀。"

"没关系,妈妈,莉莉也不认字。"

(128)

Effie: "George and I have been down-stairs in the dining-room, Mr. Mitcham. We've been playing Husband and Wife!"

Mr. Mitch: "How did you do that, my dear?"

Effie: "Why, Georgy sat at one end of the table, and I sat at the other; and Georgy said, 'This food isn't fit to eat!' and I said, 'It's all you'll get!' and Georgy said, 'Damn!' and I got up and left the room!"

埃菲:"梅彻先生,乔治和我刚才一直在楼下的餐厅里玩。我们玩过家家了。"

梅彻先生:“亲爱的,那你们是怎么玩的呢? ”

埃菲: “简单! 乔治坐桌子的这一边,我坐另一边。乔治说,‘这饭简直没法吃! ’我说,‘不吃也得吃!’,然后乔治说‘该死! ’我就站起来,出去了! ”

(129)

“What´s the matter, little boy?” said the kindhearted man. “Are you lost?”

“No,” was the manful answer; “I am not lost; I´m here. But I´d like to know where father and mother have wandered to.”

“怎么了, 孩子? ” 好心人问道,“你迷路了吗? ”

“没有,” 听起来像个小男子汉。“ 我没有迷路,我在这儿。不过,我想知道我的爸爸妈妈去哪了。”

(130)

Mother: “Hush! You two children are always quarrelling. Why can´t you agree once in a while?”

Georgia: "We do agree, mamma. Edith wants the largest apple and so do I."

母亲："嘘!你们两个孩子总在吵架。你们为什么就不能偶尔意见一致一回呢？"

乔治亚："妈妈，我们的意见很一致。伊迪丝想要最大的苹果，我也想要。"

（131）

A little boy, the youngest member of a large family, was taken to see his married sister´s new baby. He seemed more interested in the contents of the baby´s basket than in the baby, and after examining the pretty trifles, picked up a powder-puff. Much surprised at his discovery, and looking rather shocked, he said, "Isn´t she rather young for that sort of thing?"

有个小男孩儿被家人带去看已为人妻的姐姐刚生的小婴儿。这个小男孩儿有很多哥哥姐姐，他在家里排行最小。与婴儿相比，他似乎对婴儿摇篮里的东西更感兴趣。仔细看过摇篮里各色的婴儿用品之后，他拿起一个粉扑，这个发现显然是他没想到的。于是他非常惊讶地说："她用这种东西，是不是早了点儿？"

(132)

"Ma," exclaimed young Teddie, bursting into the house, "Mrs. Johnson said she would give me a penny if I told her what you said about her!"

"I never heard of such a thing!" answered his mother indignantly. "You're a very good boy not to have told! I wouldn't have her think I even mentioned her. Here's an apple, sonny, for being such a wise little lad!"

"I should think I am, ma! When she showed me the penny I told her that what you said was something awful, and worth sixpence at least!"

小特德冲进屋子喊道："妈妈，詹森太太说如果我告诉她你在背后说了她什么，她就给我一便士！"

"我还从来没听说过有这样的事！"妈妈气愤地说。"你没告诉她，可真是妈妈的乖儿子！我宁愿让她以为我从没有提到过她。儿子，这个苹果给你，你这个聪明的小家伙儿！"

"妈，我也认为我很聪明！她给我看那一便士的时候，我告诉她你说她的话很难听，至少值六便士。"

4. 锦囊妙计

Marvelous Ideas!

(133)

The young members of the family had been taught to be punctilious in contributing to the collection at church. One Sunday morning, when the boxes were being passed, James, aged six, ran his eye over those in the pew, and noticed that a guest of his sister had no coin in her hand. "Where is your money?" he whispered. She answered that she hadn´t any. But James was equal to the emergency:

"Here, take mine," he directed. "That´ll pay for you. I´ll get under the seat."

Which he did.

大人教导孩子们在教堂的捐助活动中要一丝不苟,认真对待。星期天的早晨,在大家传递捐助箱的时候,六岁的詹姆士环顾四周,发现他妹妹的一个朋友手里没有硬币。“你的钱呢?”他悄声问。小女孩儿回答说她没有。小詹姆士可是个能随机应变的孩子。

他对小女孩儿说："给，拿我的吧。这点硬币够你完成任务了。我钻到座位底下就行了。"

小男孩儿说到做到。

(134)

She: "The Borrows are having their wooden wedding next week. What can we give them?"

He: "We might send them a receipt for some of the money he owes me."

她："下周就是博罗夫妇的木婚纪念日了。我们该送什么礼物呢？"

他："可以把他们欠我们钱的收据送给他们。"

(135)

Two ladies in a car disputed concerning the window, and at last called the conductor as referee.

"If this window is open," one declared, "I shall catch cold, and will probably die."

"If the window is shut," the other

announced, "I shall certainly suffocate." The two glared at each other.

The conductor was at a loss, but he welcomed the words of a man with a red nose who sat near. These were:

"First, open the window, conductor. That will kill one. Next, shut it. That will kill the other. Then we can have peace."

公交车上，两位女士因为车窗开闭而吵得不可开交。最后只好叫来售票员评理。

一位女士说："如果打开这个窗子，我会感冒，很可能病死。"

另一位女士说："如果关上这个窗子，我会窒息，会被闷死。"

售票员不知如何是好。这时，旁边的一位红鼻子的男乘客出了一招，令售票员茅塞顿开。这位男士说：

"先打开窗子让一个死掉，然后关上窗户，让另一个死掉。这样我们就安宁了。"

(136)

"Now, let me see," the impecunious man demanded as he buttonholed an acquaintance, "do I owe you anything?"

"Not a penny, my dear sir," was the genial reply. "You are going about paying your little debts?"

"No, I´m going about to see if I´ve overlooked anybody? Lend me ten till Saturday."

一位经常身无分文的男子拦住一位熟人，说："喂，让我想想，我欠你钱吗？"

"一分也不欠，我亲爱的先生，"熟人亲切地回答。"难道你打算还钱吗？"

"不，我打算看看有没有漏掉谁。借我十便士，我周六还。"

(137)

A Kansas editor hit on the following gentle device for dunning delinquent subscribers to the paper:

"There i$ a little matter that $ome of our ubcriber$ have $eemingly forgotten entirely. $ome of them have made u$ many promi$e$, but have not kept them. To u$ it i$ a very important matter—it´$ nece$$ary in our bu$me$$. We are very mode$t and don´t like to $peak about $uch remi$$ne$$."

堪萨斯州的一位报纸编辑，想出了下面这样

一种委婉的方法，向拖欠订费的订户讨要报款。

“有一件小$hi 情，可能有些订户完全忘记了。他们向我们承诺了很多$hi。但$hi，却没有付诸于$hi 践。对我们来说，这件$hi 情很重要——这关系到我们$hi 业的兴$huai。我们很谦逊，不愿意直接$huo 明这件$hi 情。”

(138)

The bellboy of the Welcome Hotel has invented an ingenious system of calling sleepy guests. The other night a man left instructions that he wished to be called early. Next morning he was disturbed by a loud tattoo upon the door. “Well?” he demanded sharply. “I´ve got a message for you, sir.” Yawning until he strained his face, the guest jumped out of bed and unlocked the door. The bellboy handed him an envelope and then went away quickly. The guest opened the envelope, and took out a slip of paper bearing the words: “It´s time to get up.”

“欢迎饭店”的一个服务生发明了一种叫醒客人的独特方法。一天晚上，有个男客人留言说希望第二天早晨早点儿叫醒他。第二天早晨，巨大的敲门声将男客人吵醒。“什么事？”他尖声问道。

"有您的留言，先生。"客人打了一个大哈欠，从床上跳下来，开了门。服务生交给他一个信封，然后迅速离去。客人打开信封，取出里面的纸条，只见纸条上写着："该起床了。"

(139)

The successful financier snorted contemptuously.

"Money! pooh! there are a million ways of making money."

"But only one honest way," a listener declared.

"What way is that?" the financier demanded.

"Naturally, you wouldn´t know," was the answer.

The eminent financier was discoursing.

"The true secret of success," he said, "is to find out what the people want."

"And the next thing," someone suggested, "is to give it to them."

The financier shook his head contemptuously.

"No—to corner it."

一位成功的金融家自鸣得意地说：

"赚钱！简单！生财之道有千万条！"

“可是，只有一条是诚实之道，”一位听众说。

“那是什么道？”金融家问道。

“你自然是不会知道的。”对方回答。

杰出的金融家仍然在侃侃而谈：

“成功的真谛在于发现人们需要什么。”

“然后，”有人接着说，“就是满足他们的要求。”

金融家轻蔑地摇摇头：

“不，应该把他们的需求垄断起来。”

（140）

The eminent banker explained just how he started in business:

“I had nothing to do, and I rented an empty store, and put up a sign, Bank. As soon as I opened for business, a man dropped in, and made a deposit of two hundred dollars. The next day another man dropped in and deposited three hundred dollars. And so, sir, the third day, my confidence in the enterprise reached such a point that I put in fifty dollars of my own money.”

一位杰出的银行家这样向人们解释他的发家之路：

“那时，我没事可做，于是，我就租了一个空商店，挂了一个牌子：银行。刚一开张，就有一个人进来，存了两百美元。第二天，另外一个人进来存了三百美元。所以，先生，到了第三天，我对我的事业有了足够的信心，于是我将自己的五十美元投了进去。”

(141)

The lunatic peered over the asylum wall, and saw a man fishing from the bank of the river that ran close by. It was raining hard, which cooled the fevered brow of the lunatic and enabled him to think with great clearness. In consequence, he called down to the drenched fisherman:

"Caught anything?"

The man on the bank looked up, and shook his head glumly.

"How long you been there?" the lunatic next demanded.

"Three hours," was the answer.

The lunatic grinned hospitably, and called down an invitation:

"Come inside!"

有个精神病人偷偷地向精神病院的墙外望去，他看到一个人正在附近的河岸边钓鱼。天下着大雨，雨水让精神病人头脑异常冷静，思维也清晰起来。于是，他冲着浑身被雨水淋透的钓鱼人喊道：

“钓到什么了吗？”

岸边的人抬起头，沮丧地摇了摇。

“你在那里钓了多长时间了？” 精神病人又问。

“三个小时了。”钓鱼人回答。

精神病人咧着嘴，友好地邀请道：

“那就到这里来吧！”

（142）

An astronomer was entertaining a Scotch friend. He showed his visitor the moon through a telescope and asked him what he thought of the satellite.

“It´s a´ rich,” replied the Scot, who was an enthusiastic golfer, “but it´s awfully full of bunkers.”

一位天文学家正在接待一位苏格兰朋友。他让朋友在望远镜里看月亮，问他感觉如何？

苏格兰人特别喜欢打高尔夫，他回答道：“很漂亮，但是，上面怎么都是沙坑。”

（143）

"If a man has a beautiful stenographer, do you suppose that will cause him to take more interest in his business?"

"I don´t know whether he will take more interest in his business, but his wife will."

"如果一个男人有一个漂亮的女速记员，你认为他会因此而对他的事业更有兴趣吗？"

"我不知道他是否会对他的事业更有兴趣，但是，他的妻子肯定会的。"

5. 原来如此

I See!

(144)

There is no doubting the strong patriotism of the schoolboy who is the hero of this tale, although he may have been weak on history. During an examination in general history, he was asked:

"Who was the first man?"

He answered proudly, even enthusiastically, without any hesitation:

"George Washington, first in war, first in peace, first in the hearts—"

But the teacher interrupted ruthlessly:

"Wrong! Adam was the first man."

The boy sniffed disgustedly.

"Oh!" he retorted. "I didn´t know you were talking about foreigners."

毫无疑问，本故事中的这个小男孩儿非常爱国，不过，他的历史知识比较差。在一次历史考试中，有这样一道题：

"谁是第一个人？"

他不假思索地回答，而且回答得很自豪，甚至有点慷慨激昂：

“乔治·华盛顿，战争第一人，和平第一人，人民心中的第一人……”

可是，老师毫不客气地打断了他：

“错！亚当才是第一人。”

男孩不屑地嗤之以鼻。

“噢！”他反驳道，“我不知道您指的是外国人。”

（145）

The humorist offered his latest invention in the way of a puzzle to the assembly of guests in the drawing-room:

"Can you name an animal that has eyes and cannot see; legs and cannot walk, but can jump as high as the Woolworth Building?"

Everybody racked his brains during a period of deep silence, and racked in vain. Finally, they gave it up and demanded the solution. The inventor of the puzzle beamed.

"The answer," he said, "is a wooden horse. It has eyes and cannot see, and legs and cannot walk."

"Yes," the company agreed. "But how

does it jump as high as the Woolworth Building?"

"The Woolworth Building," the humorist explained, "can´t jump."

客厅里，幽默大师向一群客人展示了他最新想出来的谜语。

“有一种动物，有眼看不见，有腿不能走，可是能和伍尔沃斯大楼跳得一样高，这是什么动物？”

沉默中，大家绞尽脑汁，可是毫无结果。最后，他们放弃了，要求知道谜底。谜语的发明者得意地说：

“答案就是木马。木马有眼但看不见，有腿但不能走。”

大家纷纷点头，“是呀，可是，木马怎么能和伍尔沃斯大楼跳得一样高呢？”

“因为伍尔沃斯大楼根本不会跳”，幽默家解释道。

(146)

In the party out after reed birds was a tyro at the sport. When at last he saw one of the birds walking about, he plumped down on his stomach, and took aim. A companion called to him sharply:

"You're not going to shoot the bird while it's walking?"

"No," was the firm response; "I'll wait till it stops."

一次，大家相约出去打芦鸟，其中一人是新手。刚开始一无所获，可是后来，当他终于看到一只走动的鸟，于是，就趴下来，瞄准。有一个同伴尖声对他喊：

"你不会在鸟走动的时候开枪打它吧？"

"不，我要等到它停下来再打。"

(147)

The senator from Utah was able to disarm by flattery the resentment of a woman at a reception in Washington, who upbraided him for that plurality of wives so dear to Mormon precept and practice.

"Alas, madam," the senator declared with a touch of sadness in his voice, "we are compelled in Utah to marry a number of wives."

His fair antagonist was frankly surprised.

"What do you mean?" she demanded.

The senator explained suavely:

"We have to seek there in several women the splendid qualities that here are to be found in one."

在华盛顿的一次招待会上，一位女士因为摩门教徒所崇尚的一夫多妻制指责来自犹他州的参议员。而这位参议员则通过奉承化解了这个女人对他的敌意。

"啊，夫人，"参议员不无悲伤地说，"在犹他州，我们也是不得已才娶好几个妻子的。"

他的女对头显然很是吃惊。

"你什么意思？"她问。

议员温和地解释说：

"在这里一个女人身上能够找到的优点，在犹他州，要找好几个女人才能拥有。"

(148)

"Why is it you never get to the office on time in the morning?" demanded the boss angrily.

"It´s like this, boss," explained the tardy one; "you kept telling me not to watch the clock during office hours, and I got so I didn´t watch it at home either."

老板生气地质问员工："为什么你早晨总不能按时上班？"

迟钝的员工这样回答："老板，是这样的，你总是要求我上班的时候不要看钟表，所以，我习惯了，在家里也不看钟表。”

(149)

An English mother was visiting her son at college.

"Well, dear," she said, "what languages did you decide to take?"

"I have decided to take Pictish, mother," he replied.

"Pictish?" said the puzzled lady. "Why Pictish?"

"Only five words of it remain," he said.

一位英国母亲来看望上大学的儿子。

“亲爱的，”她问，“你打算学什么语言？”

“我决定学习皮克特语，”儿子回答。

“皮克特语？”母亲迷惑不解地问，“为什么选皮克特语？”

儿子说，“因为这种语言只剩下5个单词了。”

(150)

It was the usual domestic storm.

"Oh, dear! oh, dear!" moaned wife in tears. "I wish I´d taken poor mother´s advice, and never married you!"

Hubby, the strong, silent man, swung round on her quickly, and at last found voice.

"Did your mother try to stop you marrying me?" he demanded.

Wife nodded violently.

A look of deep remorse crossed hubby´s face.

"Great Scott," he cried, in broken tones, "how I wronged that woman!"

这是一幕常见的家庭风暴：

"噢，天哪！"妻子一把鼻涕一把泪地哭喊着，"我当初怎么不听我妈的劝，非要嫁给你！"

身强体壮，沉默寡言的丈夫，猛地回转身，半天才说出话来：

"你妈当初不想让你和我结婚？"

妻子使劲地点头。

丈夫的脸上露出深深的懊悔。

"天哪！"他痛不欲生地喊道，"我错怪了那个女人了！"

(151)

"It was a case of love at first sight when I met Jack."

"Then why didn´t you marry him?"

"I met him again so often."

"我和杰克属于一见钟情。"

"那为什么不和他结婚？"

"因为我经常和他再次见面。"

(152)

It is quite possible to trap clergymen, as well as laymen, with the following question, because they are not always learned in the Old Testament.

"If David was the father of Solomon, and Joab was the son of Zeruiah, what relation was Zeruiah to Joab?"

Most persons give the answer that Zeruiah was the father of Joab, necessarily. That is not the correct answer. The trouble is that Zeruiah was a woman. And, of course, David and Solomon having nothing whatever to do with the case.

无论是教士还是外行，对《旧约全书》都不是特别精通。因此，下面这个问题常常把他们考住：

“如果大卫是所罗门的父亲，约亚是洗鲁亚的儿子，那么洗鲁亚和约亚是什么关系？”

大多数人都回答说洗鲁亚是约亚的父亲。错！问题在于，洗鲁亚是个女的。而且，大卫和所罗门与问题的答案其实毫无关系。

（153）

London shop said:

“They are fresh which has a hen on them.”

“But I don´t see any hen.”

The clerk explained patiently.

“Not the fowl, mum, but the letter hen. Hen stands for new-laid.”

顾客要买鲜鸡蛋，伦敦店里的店员说：

“上面有‘母鸡’的蛋是鲜蛋。”

“可是，我怎么没看见母鸡。”

店员耐心地解释说：

“不是真的母鸡，而是‘母鸡’两个字。‘母鸡’就是‘鲜蛋’的意思。”

(154)

The wives of the savage chief questioned the wife of the missionary:

"And you never let your husband beat you?"

"Certainly not," the Christian lady replied. "Why, he wouldn´t dare to try such a thing!"

The oldest wife nodded understandingly.

"It is plain enough why the foreign devil has only one wife."

原始部落首领的妻妾们问传教士的妻子：

"你从来不许你的丈夫殴打你吗？"

"当然不许。"信奉基督教的女士回答。"再说了，他也不敢呀！"

部落里最年长的妇人表示非常理解：

"现在就明白了，为什么那些外来的恶魔只有一个老婆。"

(155)

The lawyer for the defense, in the damage suit, asked the witness who had seen the plaintive struck by the automobile, how far the victim was thrown by the impact.

"Fifteen feet, six and three -quarter

inches," was the instant response.

"You seem to be very exact in your figures," exclaimed the lawyer sarcastically. "How does that happen?"

"I guessed some fool lawyer would ask me," the witness answered, "and I measured the distance."

在损坏赔偿诉讼中，被告辩护律师询问车祸目击证人，受害人被车撞出多远。

"十五英尺，六又四分之三英寸，"答案脱口而出。

"您所提供的数据怎么会这么精确呢？"律师不无讽刺地质疑道。

"因为我已经猜到会有个傻瓜律师问我，"目击证人回答，"所以，我特意测量了一下。"

(156)

"How do countries come to go to war?" the little boy inquired, looking up from his book.

"For various reasons," explained the father. "Now, there was Germany and Russia. They went to war because the Russians mobilized."

"Not at all, my dear," the wife

interrupted. "It was because the Austrians—"

"Tut, tut, my love!" the husband remonstrated. "Don´t you suppose I know?"

"Certainly not—you are all wrong. It was because—"

"Mrs. Perkins, I tell you it was because—"

"Benjamin, you ought to know better, you have boggled—"

"Your opinion, madam, has not been requested in this matter."

"Shut up! I won´t have my child mistaught by an ignoramus."

"Don´t you dare, you impudent—"

"And don´t you dare bristle at me, or I´ll—"

"Oh, never mind!" the little boy intervened. "I think I know now how wars begin."

正在看书的小男孩儿抬起头问他的爸爸妈妈:"国家之间为什么要打仗?"

父亲解释说:"原因很多,比如德国和俄罗斯,他们打仗是因为俄罗斯搞军备活动。"

母亲打断了父亲的话:"根本不是这样的,他们打仗是因为奥地利——"

"嘘, 亲爱的," 丈夫反驳道:"你以为我不懂?"

"当然了,你说的不对,他们打仗是因为——"

"博金斯夫人,我告诉你他们打仗是因为——"

"本杰明,你应该聪明点,你根本不知道——"

“夫人，在这件事情上，并没有人要你发表意见。”

“闭嘴！我可不想让一个愚昧无知的人教导我的孩子。”

“不许如此放肆——”

“你也别想大发雷霆，要不我——”

这时小男孩儿说话了：“哦，算了！我现在知道为什么会打仗了。”

（157）

She: “I´m so glad we´re engaged.”

He: “But you knew all the time that I loved you, didn´t you?”

She: “Yes, dear, I knew it, but you didn´t.”

她：“我们终于订婚了，我好高兴！”

他：“我爱你，你不是一直都知道吗？”

她：“亲爱的，我当然知道，可你却不知道。”

(158)

A young couple that had received many valuable wedding presents established their home in a suburb. One morning they received in the mail two tickets for a popular show in the city, with a single line:

"Guess who sent them."

The pair had much amusement in trying to identify the donor, but failed in the effort. They duly attended the theatre, and had a delightful time. On their return home late at night, still trying to guess the identity of the unknown host, they found the house stripped of every article of value. And on the bare table in the dining-room was a piece of paper on which was written in the same hand as the enclosure with the tickets:

"Now you know!"

一对住在郊区的年轻夫妻结婚时收到许多昂贵的礼物。一天清晨,他们收到一封信,信里有两张时下正流行的演出票,还附了一句话:"猜猜谁送的?"

这道"猜人"题目着实给了夫妻俩一番乐趣,可是他们绞尽脑汁也没猜出答案。夫妻二人如期去剧院看了演出,度过了一段美好的时光。夜深人静,他们走在回家的路上仍旧在苦思冥想那个不知名的送票人究竟是谁。到家后,他们终于找到了答案。房子里所有值钱的东西都不见了,精光的餐桌上放着一张纸条,上面的笔迹与送票信上的相同:

"现在知道是谁了吧!"

(159)

George: "Why don't Jack and Laura make up?"

Kate: "'Sh! They'd like to, but unfortunately they can't remember what they quarreled about."

乔治："杰克和劳拉为什么不和好？"

凯特："嘘！他们倒是想和好的，可是，很不幸，他们忘了为什么吵架了。"

(160)

"This theory about fish being brain food is all nonsense."

"Why do you say so?"

"Because the greatest number of fish are eaten by the very people who are idiots enough to sit out all day waiting for them to bite."

"谁说鱼是补脑食物？简直是胡说八道。"

"你为什么这么说？"

"吃鱼最多的人是那些整天坐等鱼上钩的白痴。"

(161)

He: "I understand that she fairly threw herself at him."

She: "Yes! They met in an automobile collision."

他："我知道是她扑进了他的怀抱。"

她："没错！他们是在汽车相撞中认识的。"

(162)

"What's the matter with Smith? Got lumbago or spinal curvature or something?"

"No; he has to walk that way to fit some shirts his wife made for him."

"史密斯今天怎么了？腰痛还是颈椎出问题了？"

"都不是，他必须那样走路，他老婆给他做的衣服才合适。"

(163)

"Why are they not speaking?"

"They quarreled about which loved the other the more."

"Well!"

"And now each is afraid to give in for fear of offending the other."

"他们怎么不吱声了？"

"因为他们在为谁更爱对方吵架。"

"那又怎么样？"

"现在，他们都担心自己一旦让步就会伤害对方。"

(164)

Mother: "What! Have you been fighting again, Johnnie? Good little boys don´t fight."

Johnnie: "Yes, I know that. I thought he was a good little boy, but after I hit him once, I found he wasn´t."

妈妈："什么！小家伙，你又打架了？好孩子是不打架的。"

约翰尼："是的，我知道。我以为他是个好孩子，但打了他一下之后，我发现他不是。"

（165）

Husband: "What was that you were playing, my dear?"

Wife: "Did you like it?"

"It was lovely—the melody divine, the harmony exquisite!"

"It is the very thing I played last evening, and you said it was horrid."

"Well, the steak was burnt last evening."

丈夫："亲爱的，你放的是什么曲子？"

妻子："好听吗？"

"很好听——旋律很美，和弦也不错！"

"昨天晚上我放的就是这首乐曲，可是当时你却说很难听。"

"那是因为昨天的牛排烧糊了。"

（166）

The swain and his swainess had just encountered a bulldog that looked as if his bite might be quite as bad as his bark. "Why, Percy," she exclaimed as he started a strategic retreat, "you always swore you would face death for me." "I would," he flung back over his shoulder, "but that dark dog isn´t dead."

乡下，一对情侣路遇一条牛头犬，该犬龇牙咧嘴、狂吠不已，甚是凶猛可怕。

情郎哥情急之下，来了个战略性的撤退。这时，情妹妹喊道：“喂，珀西，你不是说为了我，宁愿面对死亡也在所不辞吗？”

“没错，”他回头喊道：“可是，这条黑狗是活的。”

(167)

“You say you doted on your last mistress?”

“Yes, mum. I certainly did.”

“Then why did you leave her?”

“We couldn´t continue to be friends on my wages, mum.”

“你说你很喜欢你的上一个情人？”

“是的，我的确很喜欢她。”

“那你为什么要离开她？”

“妈妈，我不能总拿我的工资和她做朋友。”

(168)

The best man noticed that one of the wedding guests, a gloomy-looking young man, did not seem to be enjoying himself. He was wandering about as though he had lost his last friend. The best man took it upon himself to cheer him up.

"Er—have you kissed the bride?" he asked by way of introduction.

"Not lately," replied the gloomy one, with a faraway expression.

婚礼上，男傧相发现一个来参加婚礼的年轻人情绪低落，很不开心。他徘徊着，好像刚刚失去了最后的朋友。男傧相走到年轻人跟前，想逗他开心。

"呃——你亲吻过新娘了吗？"他想以此打开话题。

"最近没有。"情绪低落的年轻人神情恍惚地回答。

(169)

The new vicar was paying a visit amongst the patients in the local hospital. When he entered Ward No. 2, he came across a pale-looking man lying in a cot, heavily swathed in bandages. There he stopped, and after administering a few words of comfort to the unfortunate sufferer, he remarked in cheering tones:

"Never mind, my man, you´ll soon be all right. Keep on smiling; that´s the way in the world."

"I shall never smile again," replied the youth, sadly.

"Nonsense!" ejaculated the vicar.

"There is no nonsense about it!" exclaimed the other, heatedly. "It´s through smiling at another chap´s girl that I´m here now."

新来的牧师来拜访当地的一家医院。来到二号病房的时候，他看到一个面色苍白的男子躺在帆布床上，浑身缠满了绷带。于是，他来到床前，安慰了不幸的病人一通，然后语调轻松地说：

"没关系，你很快就会好的。微笑吧，生活本该是这样的。"

"我再也不微笑了。"年轻人回答，显得很悲伤。

"胡说八道！"牧师脱口而出。

"根本没有胡说八道！"年轻人也很激动。"我躺在这里，就是因为我冲着一个小伙子的女朋友微笑了。"

(170)

Coming to a river with which he was unfamiliar, a traveler asked a youngster if it was deep.

"No," replied the boy, and the rider started to cross, but soon found that he and his horse had to swim for their lives.

When the traveler reached the other side he turned and shouted: "I thought you said it wasn´t deep?"

"It isn´t," was the reply; "it only takes grandfather´s ducks up to their middles!"

一个旅行者来到一条陌生的河边，他问一个小孩儿河水深不深。小男孩儿回答说不深。

于是，旅行者骑着马开始过河，可是很快，他就发现他和他的马为了活命不得不游过河去。

旅行者到达河对岸后，回过头冲着小男孩儿喊道："你不是说河水不深吗？"

"就是不深，爷爷家的鸭子露出一半身子就过河了。"

6. 话里有话

More Than What Is Said

(171)

"Is it true that since you came up here you´ve got engaged to Billy, Ed, George and Harry, as well as me?"

The young lady assumed an air of disdain. "What is that to you?" she demanded.

"Just this," he replied gently. "If it´s so, and you have no objection, we fellows will all chip in together to buy an engagement ring."

一个小伙子在度假时，和一个漂亮姑娘订了婚。他听到一些流言蜚语，于是就去质问这个女孩儿：

"听说你到这里以后，除了和我订婚，还和比尔，埃德，乔治，哈利订了婚。是真的吗？"

姑娘摆出一副不屑的神态，反问道：

"那又怎么样？"

"是这样的，"小伙子温和地回答说，"如果真是这样，你不反对的话，我们几个打算凑钱给你买一个订婚戒指。"

(172)

The housewife gave the tramp a large piece of pie on condition that he should saw some wood. The tramp retired to the woodshed, but presently he reappeared at the back door of the house with the piece of pie still intact save for one mouthful bitten from the end.

"Madam," he said respectfully to the wondering woman, "if it´s all the same to you, I´ll eat the wood, and saw the pie."

一位家庭主妇给了流浪汉一块馅饼，但是要求他去锯一些木柴。流浪汉拿着馅饼去了柴火房，不过很快就转身回来了。他手里还拿着那块馅饼，只咬了一口，几乎没动。

正当女主人纳闷之时，流浪汉毕恭毕敬地开口道：

"夫人，如果您不介意，我想吃掉木柴，而改锯这个馅饼。"

(173)

A member of the faculty in a London medical college was appointed an honorary physician to the king. He proudly wrote a notice, on the blackboard in his classroom:

"Professor Jennings informs his students

that he has been appointed honorary physician to His Majesty, King George."

When he returned to the classroom in the afternoon he found written below his notice this line:

"God save the King."

伦敦一所医科大学的教授被任命为国王的私人医生。他在教室的黑板上骄傲地写道：

"特此通知詹尼斯教授已被任命为国王陛下的御医。"

下午，他回到教室时，发现通知底下多了一行字：

"上帝呀，救救我们的国王！"

(174)

The new play was a failure. After the first act, many left the theatre; at the end of the second, most of the others started out. A cynical critic as he rose from his aisle seat raised a restraining hand.

"Wait!" he commanded loudly. "Women and children first!"

新戏的上演宣告失败。第一幕结束的时候，不少人离开了剧院。第二幕结束的时候，大多数人开始离席。一位喜欢讽刺挖苦的剧评家从靠近过道的座位上站起来，举着手，做制止状：

“等等！妇女儿童优先！”

(175)

The naked hills lie wanton to the breeze,
The fields are nude, the groves unfrocked,
Bare are the shivering limbs of shameless trees,
What wonder is it that the corn is shocked!
But not the modern woman!

裸露的山丘在微风中肆无忌惮地躺着，
田野裸露着，小树林也脱去了上衣，
赤裸的，还有那些毫无羞耻之心的树枝，
难怪玉米如此震惊！
如今的女人却不会震惊！

(176)

An eminent statesman was being driven rapidly by his chauffeur, when the car struck and killed a dog that leaped in front of it. At the statesman's order, the chauffeur stopped the car, and the great man got out and hurried back to where a woman was standing by the remains. The dead dog´s mistress was deeply grieved, and more deeply angered. As the statesman attempted to address her placatingly, she turned on him wrathfully, and told him just what she thought, which was considerable and by no means agreeable. When, at last, she paused for breath, the culprit tried again to soothe her, saying:

"Madam, I shall be glad to replace your dog."

The woman drew herself up haughtily, surveyed the statesman with supreme scorn, and hissed:

"Sir, you flatter yourself!"

一辆车快速行驶在马路上，车上载着一位著名的政治家。突然，一条狗跳到车前，被当场压死了。政治家让司机停车，然后赶紧下车走向站在死狗身旁的女士。狗的女主人非常悲伤，而且非常愤怒。政治家试图安慰她，可是她愤怒至极，指着他痛骂起来。当然，话很难听。最后，在她停下来歇口气的时候，政治家又一次安慰她道："夫人，我很愿意赔偿(replace)你的狗。"

这位女士傲慢地挺了挺身子，非常轻蔑地打量了一下政治家，从牙缝里挤出了这样一句话：

"先生，你也太高看自己了。"

（注：replace 还有一个意思就是"替代，代替"。）

(177)

The woman, who had a turn-up nose and was somewhat self-conscious concerning it, bought a new pug dog, and petted it so fondly as to excite the jealousy of her little daughter.

"How do you like your new little brother?" she asked the child teasingly.

The girl replied, rather maliciously, perhaps:

"He looks just like his mother."

一个女人对自己有点儿上翘的鼻子相当敏感。她买回来一只哈巴狗,并对它宠爱之至,这引起了小女儿的不满。

一次她开玩笑地问女儿:"你觉得你的新弟弟怎么样?"

小女孩儿的回答也许并非有意,但却相当恶毒:

"他长得很像妈妈。"

(178)

"Did your late employer give you a testimonial, Jack?"

"Yes, Tom. But the way employers look at it when I apply for a job make one think there's something wrong with it."

"What does it say, then?"

"Why, he said I was one of the best men his firm had ever turned out."

"杰克，你的前一任老板给你写推荐信了吗？"

"写了，可是，我去找工作的时候，那些老板看推荐信的样子总让人觉得什么地方不对劲儿。"

"那么推荐信是怎么说的？"

"他说，我是他公司辞退的最优秀的员工之一。"

(179)

Wife: "George, is that you?"

George: "Why certainly! Who else you are expecting at this time of the night?"

妻子："乔治，是你吗？"

乔治："当然！半夜这个时候，你还以为会是谁？"

（180）

A well –known millionaire entertained Edward Everett Hale with other guests at a dinner. The host was not only hospitable, but wished every one to know his liberality. During the meal, he extolled the various viands, and did not hesitate to give their value in dollars and cents. In speaking of some very beautiful grapes served, which had been grown on his estate, he wearied the company by a careful calculation as to just how much a stem of them had cost him. Doctor Hale grinned pleasantly as he extended his empty plate, with the request:

"I´ll thank you to cut me off about $1.87 worth more, please."

一位有名的百万富翁设宴招待美国著名的作家爱德华·埃弗里特·黑尔，在座的还有其他几位客人。男主人热情好客，而且乐于让在座的每一位客人都了解他的慷慨大方。席间，他对各种珍馐美味赞不绝口，而且还迫不及待地将这些美食的价格一一详细报出。桌上有他在自家园子里种植的精美葡萄，他不厌其烦地向在座的客人仔细计算了每一串葡萄的成本。对此，黑尔博士举起自己的空盘子，咧开嘴愉快地笑着央求道：

"请再给我切价值约 1.87 美元的葡萄，谢谢！"

(181)

The little girl in the car was a pest. She crossed the aisle to devote herself to a dignified fat man, to his great annoyance. She asked innumerable questions, and, incidentally, counted aloud his vest buttons to learn whether he was rich man, poor man, beggar man or thief. The mother regarded the child´s efforts as highly entertaining. The fat man leaned forward and addressed the lady very courteously:

"Madam, what do you call this dear little child?"

"Ethel," the beaming mother replied.

"Please call her then," the fat man requested.

车厢里的小女孩儿可真是个小讨厌。她穿过过道来到一位不苟言笑的胖绅士面前，这让绅士很烦。小女孩儿向他提了无数的问题，然后，就开始大声地数他衣服上的纽扣，想看看他是富人，还是穷人，是乞丐还是小偷。孩子的妈妈看着孩子的举动，觉得很好玩。这时，发福的绅士向前靠了靠，很礼貌地问女士：

"夫人，请问您怎么叫这个小宝贝儿？"

"埃塞尔，"妈妈愉快地回答。

"那么就请您叫叫她吧，"绅士说。

(182)

The playwright rushed up to the critic at the club.

"I've had a terrible misfortune," he announced. "My little three-year-old boy got at my new play, and tore it all to pieces."

"Extraordinary that a child so young should be able to read," said the critic.

剧作家冲进俱乐部,对评论家说。

"今天真倒霉,我三岁的小儿子看了我新写的剧本,把它撕成碎片了。"

"这么小的孩子,就能读懂剧本,真不简单呀!"评论家说。

(183)

"Did you hear about the awful trouble that has befallen Mrs. Talkalot?"

"Don't tell me she has lost her voice."

"No, her husband has lost his hearing."

"你听说了吗?塔尔卡罗遭遇不幸了。"

"别告诉我她失声了。"

"不是的,是她丈夫失聪了。"

(184)

"Do you think I shall live until I´m ninety, doctor?"

"How old are you now?"

"Forty."

"Do you drink, gamble, smoke, or have you any vices of any kind?"

"No. I don´t drink, I never gamble, I loathe smoking; in fact, I haven´t any vices."

"Well, good heavens, what do you want to live another fifty years for?"

"医生,你说我能活到九十岁吗?"

"你现在多大?"

"四十。"

"你喝酒吗?赌博吗?抽烟吗?一句话,你有没有什么不良嗜好?"

"没有,我不喝酒,不赌博,我讨厌抽烟,事实上,我什么不良嗜好也没有。"

"天哪,那你再活五十年干什么呢?"

(185)

"His versatility is something extra-ordinary."

"I had an idea he was rather stupid."

"That´s just it. I never met a man who could make more different kinds of a fool of himself."

"他真是多才多艺啊！"

"可我觉得他很笨。"

"我说的就是这个意思。我从来没见过他这样的人，在各种场合都能把自己变成傻瓜。"

(186)

Julia: "Fanny married a very wealthy man, you know. She tells me she has absolutely nothing to wish for."

Gertrude: "Oh, Julia! What a dreadful state to be in."

朱莉娅："你知道的，范妮嫁给了一个有钱人。她告诉我说她现在别无所求了。"

格特鲁德："噢，天哪！那太可怕了！"

(187)

"She is one of the most remarkable women I ever met."

"In what way?"

"She can keep silence in four different

languages."

"她是我见过的最了不起的女人之一。"

"为什么？"

"因为她可以用四种语言保持沉默。"

(188)

The young man at the summer resort, who had become engaged to the pretty girl, received information that led him to question her:

The young lady, who was something of a food faddist, was on a visit to a coast fishing village. She questioned her host as to the general diet of the natives, and was told that they subsisted almost entirely on fish. The girl protested:

"But fish is a brain food, and these folks are really the most unintelligent-looking that I ever saw."

"Mebbe so," the host agreed. "And just think what they'd look like if they didn't eat fish!"

一位喜欢研究食物的年轻女士来到一个小渔村，借住在一个渔民家里。她向主人讨教当地人以何为食。主人说他们基本上以鱼为食。年轻的女士质疑道：

“鱼是养脑的食物，可是，这些渔民是我所见过的最愚钝的人了。”

“也许吧，”主人表示赞同。“可想而知，如果他们不吃鱼的话，会是什么样子！”

(189)

The energetic New England woman addressed her hired girl in a discouraged tone:

"Here it is Monday morning and to-morrow will be Tuesday, and the next day Wednesday—the whole week half gone, and nothing done yet!"

精力充沛的新英格兰女人不满地教训女佣说：

“看，今天是星期一早晨，明天就是星期二，后天星期三——半周都过去了，可什么都没做！”

(190)

The wife: "I have not been able to wear my new hat yet on account of the weather."

The husband: "Humph! And I suppose by the time it clears up the fashion will have changed."

妻子:"因为天气总不合适，我一直都没有机会戴我的新帽子。"

丈夫:"哼！我想,等天晴的时候,你的帽子也过时了。"

(191)

"I really believe he married her only because he wanted a good housekeeper."

"And now I suppose he wishes he could give her a month´s warning."

"我敢肯定他娶她只是想让她当管家。"

"我想现在他巴不得她一个月后离职。"

(192)

"The way those people flaunt their money fairly makes me ill."

"Sour grapes always did have that effect."

"那些炫耀自己有钱的人真让我恶心。"

"这就是酸葡萄效应。"

(193)

Wife: “Yes, dear. I thought I´d buy you something you´d never think of buying for yourself.”

Husband (as he gazes with horror at the canary-colored socks): “Yes, dear, and you have succeeded.”

妻子:“亲爱的,我给你买了一件东西,一件你自己永远都不会想到要买的东西。”

丈夫(他用恐惧的目光注视着淡黄色的袜子):“是的,亲爱的,你说得一点儿没错。”

(194)

“That gentleman who is being introduced to Miss Binks is a free thinker.”

“Which is he, a bachelor or a widower?”

“介绍给宾客斯小姐的那位男士是一个自由的思想家。”

“噢,他是单身汉还是鳏夫?”

(195)

"Some wise person once said that silence was golden, did he not?"

"I believe so. Why?"

"I was just thinking how extravagant some women are."

"是不是曾经有智者说过沉默是金？"

"是的，怎么了？"

"我在想有些女人太奢侈了。"

(196)

The Escort: Who´s that fellow who seems to know you?

The Lady: Only a second cousin once removed.

The Escort: Hm! Well, he looks as if he wanted removing again.

护花使者：那个家伙是谁？他好像认识你。

女士：不过是一个远房侄子，已经搬到别处去了。

护花使者：哦，看样子他又想搬回来了。

(197)

The son of the family was home on his first vacation since he had attained to the dignity of college prefect. He and his father were discussing affairs of the day, and finally the boy remarked: "Say, Guv, I hope when I am as old as you are, I'll know more than you do."

"I'll go you one better, my boy," the father replied. "I hope that when you are that old you will know as much as you think you do now."

儿子考上一所好大学，第一次放假回家。一天，父子俩闲聊，聊到最后儿子说："嘿，老爸，我希望我到您这个岁数的时候，能懂得比您还多。"

"儿子，我希望你比我强，"父亲回答说。"我希望到那个时候，你懂的知识，能和你现在自以为已经懂的一样多。"

(198)

A woman who had visited every department of one of the big London shops and worried the majority of the salesmen without spending a penny, so exasperated one of them that he ventured to make a mild protest. "Madam," he asked, "are you shopping here?"

The lady looked surprised, but not by any means annoyed. "Certainly!" she replied. "What else should I be doing?"

For a moment the salesman hesitated; then he blurted out, "Well, madam, I thought perhaps you were taking an inventory!"

伦敦一家大商场里，一位女士逛遍每一个柜台，却没花一分钱，这让大部分售货员都很不满意。有一名售货员实在忍不住了，他走上前礼貌地抗议道："太太，您是来这里购物的吗？"女士很吃惊，但并没有生气："当然！"她回答。"你以为我来这里做什么？"

这个售货员犹豫了一会儿，然后脱口而出："哦，太太，我还以为您在这里清点商品呢！"

(199)

Lawyer: "When I was a boy my highest ambition was to be a pirate."

Client: "You're in luck. It isn't every man who can realize the dreams of his youth."

律师："小时候，我最大的梦想就是当一个海盗。"

客户:“你真走运。不是所有的人都能实现年轻时候的梦想的。”

(200)

Dad (sternly): Where were you last night?

Son: Oh, just riding around with some of the boys.

Dad: Well, tell them not to leave their hairpins in the car.

爸爸(严厉地):昨晚你去哪儿了?

儿子:哦,和别的男同学一起开车去兜了兜风。

爸爸:那么,告诉他们不要把发夹丢在车里。

(201)

She: “And what would you be now if it weren´t for my money?”

He: “A bachelor.”

她:“如果不是我的钱,你现在会是什么?”

他:“单身汉。”

(202)

There was a distinct air of chastened resignation about him, as he penned the following note:

"Dear Miss Brown,—I return herewith your kind note in which you accept my offer of marriage. I would draw your attention to the fact that it begins 'Dear George.' I do not know who George is, but my name, as you will remember, is Thomas."

他在书写下面这个留言的时候，显然是下定了放弃的决心。

"亲爱的布朗小姐，您的回信我已经收到了，承蒙您的厚爱接受了我的求婚。不过，我想提请您注意您的信开头的称呼是'亲爱的乔治'。我不知道乔治是谁，但是，我的名字，如果您还记得的话，是托马斯。"

(203)

Screen Actress: I have a certificate from my doctor saying that I cannot act to-day.

Manager: Why did you go to all that trouble? I could have given you a certificate saying that you never could act.

电影演员：我这里有医生开的证明，证明我今天不能拍戏。

经理：何必那么麻烦？我本来也可以给你开一个证明，证明你再也不能拍戏了。

7. 针锋相对

Tit for Tat

(204)

"Would you like a lock of my hair?" asked the gallant old bachelor of the spinster who had been a belle a few decades past.

"Why don´t you offer me the whole wig?" the maiden lady gibed, with a titter.

The bachelor retorted with icy disdain:

"You are very biting, madam, considering that your teeth are porcelain."

"我送你一缕我的头发怎么样？"一位多年前的单身美女问另一位终身未婚的女人。

"你何不把整个假发套都送给我呢？"终身未婚的女人窃笑着嘲讽道。

老美女毫不留情地回击道：

"女士，你的嘴巴还挺厉害嘛，虽然是满口烤瓷牙。"

(205)

Phil May, the artist, when once down on his luck in Australia, took a job as waiter in a very low-class restaurant. An acquaintance came into the place to dine, and was aghast when he discovered the artist in his waiter.

"My God!" he whispered. "To find you in such a place as this."

Phil May smiled, as he retorted:

"Oh, but, you see, I don't eat here."

艺术家麦菲尔在命运不济的时候，曾经在澳大利亚的一个小餐馆打工。一次，麦菲尔的一位熟人来这家小餐馆吃饭。当他认出跑堂的竟然是大艺术家麦菲尔时，着实吃惊不小。

"天哪！"他低声说。"怎么在这么破的地方见到你。"

麦菲尔微笑着，回答说：

"是呀，不过，你看，我不在这里用餐。"

(206)

It was a late hour when the hostess at the reception requested the eminent basso to sing.

"It is too late, madam," he protested. "I should disturb your neighbors."

"Not at all," declared the lady, beaming.

"Besides, they poisoned our dog last week."

时间已经很晚了，宴会女主人还是请求有名的男低音歌唱家唱上一曲。

歌唱家说："太晚了，夫人，会打扰您的邻居的。"

"没关系，"女主人幸灾乐祸地说。"谁让上周他们把我家的狗给毒死了。"

(207)

The prize bull-dog attacked a farmer, who defended himself with a pitchfork, and in doing so killed the dog. The owner was greatly distressed, and reproached the farmer.

"Why didn´t you use the other end of the fork," he demanded, "and just beat him off, without killing him?"

"I would have," the farmer answered, "if he had come at me with the other end."

一只金牌斗牛犬向一个农夫冲去，情急之下，农夫拿起一个干草叉进行防卫，结果把狗叉死了。狗主人很伤心，责备农夫说：

"你为什么不用叉子的另一头？把它赶走就行了，为什么杀死它？"

"我本来想用另一头来着，"农夫回答，"可是您的狗却没有用另一头冲向我。"

(208)

"Darling," he asked, as he drew his fiancée closer to him, "am I the first man you have ever kissed?"

"William," replied the American girl, somewhat testily, "before we go any further I would like to ask you a few questions. You are, no doubt, fully aware that my father is a millionaire something like ten times over, aren´t you?"

"Y-yes."

"You understand, no doubt, that when he dies all of his vast fortune will be left to me?"

"Y-yes."

"You know that I have a quarter of a million dollars in cash in my name at the bank?"

"Y-yes."

"And own two and a half million dollars´ worth of property?"

"Y-yes."

"That my diamonds are insured to the value of a quarter of a million dollars?"

"Y-yes."

"My horses and motor-cars are worth seventy-five thousand dollars?"

"Y-yes."

"Then, for goodness´ sake, talk sense! What difference would it make to you if I had been kissed by a thousand men before I met you?"

“亲爱的，” 他把未婚妻拉过来一点儿，问道：“我是你第一个亲吻过的男人吗？”

“威廉，”美国女孩回应道，显然有些不高兴。“回答你的问题之前，我想问你几个问题。你肯定清楚我爸爸是个超级百万富翁，对吧？”

“是的。”

“你肯定也明白他去世后，他的大笔财产都会留给我，对吧？”

“是的。”

“你知道银行里我名下的现金存款有二十五万美元，对吧？”

“是的。”

“而且你也知道我还拥有价值二百五十万美元的财产，对吧？”

“是的。”

“你肯定还知道我的钻石投保总价是二十五万美元，对吧？”

“是的。”

“你也知道我的马和汽车价值七万五千美元，对吧？”

“是的。”

“那么，看在上帝的分上，说话的时候，要面对现实。如果在你之前，我得到过上千个男人的亲吻，那又怎样？”

(209)

The man sitting in the street car addressed the woman standing before him:

"You must excuse my not giving you my seat—I'm a member of the Sit Still Club."

"Certainly, sir," the woman replied. "And please excuse my staring—I belong to the Stand and Stare Club."

She proved it so well that the man at last sheepishly got to his feet.

"I guess, ma'am," he mumbled, "I'll resign from my club and join yours."

公共汽车上，一位坐着的男人对站在他面前的女人说：

"请原谅我不能给您让座，因为我是静坐俱乐部的成员。"

"没关系，先生，"女人回答。"也请您原谅我盯着您看，因为我是站着盯俱乐部的成员。"

女人说到做到，以至于后来那个男人还是局促不安地站了起来。

"我想，夫人，"他咕哝着说，"我得从我的俱乐部退出，加入您的俱乐部。"

（210）

Mrs. Lynks: "Jack, I have made up my mind to fine you ten cents every time you swear."

Mr. Lynks: "That's a bargain, if you'll give me ten cents every time you envy me for being able to."

林克斯夫人："杰克，我已经决定了，以后你每诅咒发誓一次，我就罚你一毛钱。"

林克斯先生："就这么定了，以后你要是再埋怨我赌咒发誓，你就给我一毛钱。"

（211）

The great pugilist was superstitious and fond of lobster. When the waiter served one with a claw missing, he protested. The waiter explained that this lobster had been worsted in a fight with another in the kitchen. The great pugilist pushed back his plate.

"Carry him off," he commanded, "and bring me the winner."

一位了不起的拳击家很迷信。他喜欢吃龙虾。有一次，服务生端上来的龙虾少了一个爪子，他很不满意。服务生解释说，这个龙虾之所以残缺不全，是因为在厨房里，和另一个龙虾打架输了。伟大的拳击家把盘子推到一边，命令道：

"拿走，把那个胜利者给我端上来。"

(212)

Customer to Palmist: "Five dollars fee? Er—would you have any objection to waiting until I get some of the money you say is coming to me?"

顾客对算命先生说："收费5美元？唔——您不是说我很快就会发一笔小财吗？那么等我拿到那笔钱的时候再付您钱，您不介意吧？"

(213)

"I sincerely regret our misunderstanding, Florence, and am quite ready to be friends again."

"Misunderstanding, indeed! If you had any feeling you'd call it a quarrel."

"佛罗伦斯，对我们之间的误会我深感遗憾，我希望我们再次成为朋友。”

“误会？可笑！如果你还有良知的话，应该说那是吵架才对。”

（214）

The First Woman: “The cheek of that conductor! He glared at me as if I hadn't paid any fare.”

The Second Woman: “And what did you do?”

The First Woman: “I just glared back at him—as if I had!”

第一个女人：“别提那个售票员的脸色有多难看了！他盯着我，好像我没买票似的。”

第二个女人：“那你怎么做的呢？”

第一个女人：“我也盯着他——就好像我已经买票了。”

（215）

The Wife: “Oh, you needn't sneer! I mean every word I say.”

"I´m not sneering, my dear. I´m just thinking what a lot you must mean."

妻子:"噢,你用不着冷笑!我说的每句话都是心里话。"

"我没有冷笑,亲爱的。我只是在想你的心里话可真多呀。"

(216)

The motor car was driven by a determined young woman, who had knocked down a man without injuring him much.

She did not try to get away. Instead, she stopped the car, descended to the solid earth and faced him manfully.

"I´m sorry it happened," she said grudgingly, "but it was all your fault. You must have been walking carelessly. I´m an experienced driver. I´ve been driving a car for seven years."

"Well," replied her victim angrily, "I´m not a novice myself. I´ve been walking for fifty-seven years."

一个独断专行的年轻女人开车撞倒了一位男士,但他没怎么受伤。

她没有惊慌逃离,相反,她把车停下来,走出来稳稳当当往那儿一站，无畏地面对着被撞的男士。

“对刚才的事情，我很抱歉，”她说的时候并不真诚。“但这都是你的错。你走路的时候应该小心点。我可是老司机，已经开了 7 年车了。”

“哼，”被撞的男士愤愤地回答，“我也不是新手，我已经走了 57 年的路了。”

（217）

Mrs. Murphy is very fat, and the other day, laden with parcels and packages, she was trying to mount the steps of a Dublin tramcar. Helplessly looking on, stood the conductor, a diminutive little chap.

Mrs. Murphy, having reached the platform, said, with a glance of withering scorn: “If ye was half a man ye would have helped me up.”

The little conductor calmly replied: “Sure, ma′am, if ye was half a woman I would!”

墨菲夫人很胖，有一天，在都柏林，她拿着很多的包裹和行李，想上电车。售票员是个身材瘦小的小伙子。他站在那里看着她费力地往上爬，一动也不动。

墨菲夫人好不容易上了车，她狠狠地瞪了小伙子一眼,轻蔑地说:“你哪怕是半个男人,也应该帮帮我。”

瘦弱的售票员平静地回答:“当然了,夫人,您哪怕是半个女人,我也会帮的。”

8. 对症下药

Acts Accordingly

(218)

Many a great man has been given credit as originator of this cynical sentiment:

"The more I see of men, the more I respect dogs."

据说，以下这句警世名言出自不止一位伟人之口:

"我越了解人类,就越尊敬犬类。"

(219)

A wise old Quaker woman once said that men were guilty of three most astonishing follies. The first was the climbing of trees to shake down the fruit, when if they would but wait, the fruit would fall of itself. The second was the going to war to kill one another, when if they would only wait, they must surely die naturally. The third was that they should run after women, when, if they did not do so, the women would surely run after them.

一位年长而智慧的教友派女士曾经说过，男人有三大罪。第一宗是爬上树去摇水果，其实他们应该等待水果自己掉下来；第二宗是上战场相互残杀，其实他们应该等待，那些人迟早会自然死亡；第三宗是他们追求女人，其实，如果他们不追女人的话，女人迟早会追求他们的。

(220)

The philosopher calmly defined the exact difference between life and love:

"Life is just one fool thing after another: love is just two fool things after each other."

生活和爱有何不同？以下是哲学家冷静的解释：

"生活是不同的蠢事接踵而至，而爱则是两个蠢物来来往往。"

(221)

Love is blind, but marriage is an eye-opener.

爱虽会使人变成瞎子，但婚姻会帮你重新睁开双眼。

(222)

Artemas Ward said: "When I am sad, I sing, and then others are sad with me."

19 世纪报纸专栏作家阿蒂默斯·沃德说：

"悲伤的时候，我唱歌，然后，其他人都会跟着我悲伤。"

(223)

The optimistic pessimist explained why he always dined in restaurants where music was provided.

"Because it works two ways: sometimes the music helps to make me forget the food, and sometimes the food helps to make me forget the music."

乐观的悲观主义者向人们解释为什么他总在播放音乐的餐厅吃饭：

"因为这有两方面的作用：有时候，音乐有助于我忘记食物；有时候，食物有助于我忘掉音乐。"

(224)

The Man of Theory: "The great secret of happiness lies in being content with one´s lot."

The Man of Practice: "But it has to be a whole lot."

理想主义者："幸福的秘诀在于知天命。"

现实主义者："可是，那得是很好的命才行。"

(225)

The Husband: "Why is it that women always say, ´I´ll be ready in two seconds´?"

The Wife: "Humph! and why is it that men always say, ´Oh! I´m ready now´?"

丈夫："为什么女人总是说 '再等两秒钟就好了'？"

妻子："为什么男人总是说'哦！已经好了？'"

（226）

Old Job: "The best way to get the most out of life is to fall in love with a great problem or a beautiful woman!"

Old Steve: "Why not choose the latter and get both?"

老乔布："让人生最有收获的好办法不是爱上一个大问题就是爱上一个大美女！"

老史蒂夫："为什么不选美女，这样可以两者兼得。"

（227）

The baby pulled brother's hair until he yelled from the pain of it. The mother soothed the weeping boy:

"Of course, she doesn't know how badly it hurts." Then she left the room.

She hurried back presently on hearing

frantic squalling from baby.

"What in the world is the matter with her?" she questioned anxiously.

"Nothing at all," brother replied contentedly. "Only now she knows."

小女孩揪着哥哥的头发，把哥哥痛得大叫起来。妈妈安慰着哭泣的男孩儿说：

“她肯定不知道揪头发有多疼。”说完，妈妈出去了。

她刚出门，就听到小女儿歇斯底里的尖叫。

“天哪，她怎么了？”妈妈跑回来焦急地问道。

“没事，”哥哥心满意足地回答。“不过现在她知道揪头发有多痛了。”

(228)

The advertisement offered for fifty cents a recipe by which to whiten the hands and soften them. Girls who sent the money received the following directions:

"Soak the hands three times a day in dish water while mother rests."

有一则广告说，可以提供让双手美白柔嫩的配方，收费为五十美分。那些寄了钱的女孩儿，收到的配方如下：

“把手浸泡在洗碗水中，一天三次，此时，让你的妈妈休息。”

(229)

The master directed that the picture should be hung on the east wall; the mistress preferred the west wall.

The servant drove the nail where his master directed, but when he was left alone in the room he drove a nail in the other wall.

"That," he said to himself, "will save my lugging the steps up here again to-morrow, when he has come around to agreeing with her."

男主人要把画挂在东面的墙上，而女主人则想把画挂在西面的墙上。

男仆按男主人的要求把钉子钉在了东墙上，可是，主人走后，他又把钉子改钉在了西墙上。他自我解释说：

“这样，明天男主人一觉起来听了他老婆的话，我就省得再爬上来一次了。”

(230)

Lady (to pedlar): "No, thank you, we never buy anything at the door."

Pedlar: "Then I've just the thing for you, Madam. You will, I am sure, appreciate these tasteful little 'No Pedlars' notices."

女士（对小商贩）：“不买，谢谢。我们从来不买上门推销的东西。”

小商贩：“太太，那么我这里刚好有种东西适合您。这些‘谢绝小商贩’的小标签很有品位，你肯定会喜欢。

(231)

First Theatrical Manager: "Do you have any trouble with the girl who is playing the flapper in your new show?"

Second Theatrical Manager: "No; if she attempts to be skittish I just threaten to publish the photographs of her two sons who are lieutenants in the army."

第一个舞台经理：“让你的女演员演那个轻佻女子，你是不是很难搞定？”

第二个舞台经理：“没有，如果她忸忸怩怩不愿意，我就威胁她说要公开她那两个已经是陆军中尉的儿子的照片。”

9. 自讨没趣

Ask for It

(232)

Two boys once thought to play a trick on Charles Darwin. They took the body of a centipede, the wings of a butterfly, the legs of a grasshopper and the head of a beetle, and glued these together to form a weird monster. With the composite creature in a box, they visited Darwin.

"Please, sir, will you tell us what sort of a bug this is?" the spokesman asked.

The naturalist gave a short glance at the exhibit and a long glance at the boys.

"Did it hum?" he inquired solemnly.

The boys replied enthusiastically, in one voice:

"Oh, yes, sir."

"Well, then," Darwin declared, "it is a humbug."

两个男孩儿曾经想愚弄查尔斯·达尔文。他们找来蜈蚣的身体，蝴蝶的翅膀，蚂蚱的腿，还有甲壳虫的头，用胶水把这些东西粘成了一个怪物。他们把这个怪物放在一个盒子里，去找达尔文。

“先生，您能告诉我们这是什么虫吗？”男孩儿问道。

博物学家达尔文扫了一眼他们带来的虫子，又盯着两个男孩儿看了一会儿。然后，严肃地问道：

“它嗡嗡叫吗？”

两个男孩儿异口同声、急切地回答：

“对，它嗡嗡叫。”

“那么，好吧，”达尔文宣布说：“这是嗡嗡虫（骗人虫）。”

（注：这里 hum 是双关语，hum 可以是嗡嗡叫的意思，也有骗人的意思。）

(233)

"I wish I could know how many men will be made wretched when I get married," said the languishing coquette to her most intimate confidante.

"I'll tell you," came the catty answer, "if you'll tell me how many men you're going to marry."

一个风情万种的女子对她的闺中密友说：“我真想知道如果我结婚，会有多少男人痛不欲生。”

“如果你告诉我你打算和多少男人结婚，我就告诉你答案。”女友不怀好意地说。

（234）

The eminent English Statesman Arbuthnot–Joyce plays golf so badly that he prefers a solitary round with only the caddy present. He had a new boy one day recently, and played as wretchedly as usual.

"I fancy I play the worst game in the world," he confessed to the caddy.

"Oh, I wouldn´t say that, sir," was the consoling response. "From what the boys were saying about another gentleman who plays here, he must be worse even than you are."

"What´s his name?" asked the statesman hopefully.

And the caddy replied:

"Arbuthnot–Joyce."

英国著名的政治家阿布斯诺·乔伊斯的高尔夫打得很糟。所以，他喜欢独自打球，只留一个球童在场。一天，来了一个新的球童，而乔伊斯，则一如既往，打得很糟。

"我想我是世界上高尔夫打得最糟糕的人了。"他对新球童坦言道。

"噢，可别这么说，先生，"球童安慰道，"听别的球童说，这里还有一位先生，他肯定比你打得还糟。"

"他叫什么名字？"政治家满怀希望地问道。

球童回答说：

"他叫阿布斯诺·乔伊斯。"

(235)

The kindly old lady chanced to be present at the feeding of the lions in the zoo. Presently, she remarked to the keeper:

"Isn't that a very small piece of meat to give to the lions?"

The man answered very respectfully, but firmly:

"It may seem like a very small piece of meat to you, mum, but it seems like a big piece of meat to the lions, mum."

一位仁慈的老妇人逛动物园的时候，刚好看到饲养员在喂狮子。很快，她就对饲养员说：

"那块肉对狮子来说，未免有点儿太小了吧？"

饲养员的回答很客气，但也相当有力：

"夫人，这块肉对您来说可能有点儿小了，但是，对狮子来说，已经不算小了。"

(236)

An old lady in the London parish of the famous Doctor Gill made a nuisance of herself by constant interference in the affairs of others. As a gossip she was notorious. It appeared to her that the neckbands worn by the Doctor were longer than was fitting. She therefore took occasion to visit the clergyman, and harangued him at length on the sinfulness of pride. Then she exhibited a pair of scissors, and suggested that she should cut down the offending neckbands to a size fitting her ideas of propriety. The Doctor listened patiently to her exhortation, and at the end offered her the neckbands on which to work her will. She triumphantly trimmed them to her taste, and returned the shorn remnants to the minister.

"And now," said the Doctor, "you must do me a good turn also."

"That I will, Doctor," the woman declared heartily. "What can it be?"

"Well," the clergyman explained, "you have something about you which is a deal too long and which causes me and many others such trouble, that I should like to see it shorter."

"Indeed, dear Doctor, I shall not hesitate to gratify you. What is it? See, here are the scissors! Use them as you please."

"Come, then," said the Doctor, "good sister, put out your tongue."

伦敦著名的吉尔神父的教区住着一位老妇人,她总是掺和别人的事情,很令人讨厌,是个远近闻名的长舌妇。有一次老妇人觉得神父的衬衫领子太长,不合适,于是她就找了个机会去拜访神父,在他面前大谈特谈傲慢的罪恶。然后,她拿出一把剪刀,提议说由她来将过长的衣领剪短。神父耐心地听完她的训词，然后，将衬衫领子交给她，随她处理。她得意地将衣领按照她的品位进行了修剪，最后，将修剪后的衣领交给了神父。

这时，神父开口了："现在，你也要帮我一个忙。"

"那当然了，神父，"老妇人满心欢喜地答应道。"要我做什么？"

神父说，"你身上也有一件东西太长了，让我和其他人感到不舒服，我想让它也短一点。"

"那当然了，神父，我很乐意满足您的要求。是什么东西？给您，剪刀！随便剪。"

"过来，"神父说，"好姐妹，把你的舌头伸出来。"

（237）

The First Man (to new acquaintance): "I wonder if that fat old girl is really trying to flirt with me?"

The Second Man: "I can easily find out by asking her—she is my wife."

第一个男人（对一个刚认识不久的人）："我想知道那个又老又胖的女人是不是想跟我调情？"

第二个男人："我可以帮你问问——她是我的妻子。"

(238)

Everything that could be done to make the great unemployed meeting a success had been accomplished. A large hall, and a good speaker had been engaged.

When the latter arrived he seemed in a crabby frame of mind. Looking round, he beckoned the chairman.

"I should like to have a glass of water on my table, if you please," he said.

"To drink?" was the chairman´s idiotic question.

"Oh, no," was the sarcastic retort, "when I´ve been speaking half-an-hour I do a high dive."

失业者大会的一切准备工作就绪，会议大厅已经布置停当，并且已经邀请到一位不错的发言人。

这位发言人到达的时候，看起来心情不佳。他环顾四周，向会议主席招了招手，说：

"请在我的桌子上放一杯水。"

"是喝的吗？"会议主席的问题显然非常愚蠢。

"噢，不是。"演讲者没好气地回答，"讲到半小时的时候，我要高台跳水。"

(239)

The shaded lights, music in the distance, sweet perfumes from the costly flowers about them—everything was just right for a proposal, and Tim decided to chance his luck. She was pretty, which was good, and also, he believed, an heiress, which was better.

"Are you not afraid that someone will marry you for your money?" he asked gently.

"Oh! dear, no," smiled the girl. "Such an idea never entered my head!"

"Ah! Miss Lisa," he sighed, "in your sweet innocence you do not dream how coldly, cruelly mercenary some men are!"

"Perhaps I don't," replied the girl calmly.

"I would not for a moment have such a terrible fate befall you," he said passionately. "You are too good—too beautiful. The man who wins you should love you for yourself alone."

"He'll have to," the girl remarked. "It's my cousin Jennie who has the money—not I. You seem to have got us mixed. I haven't a penny myself."

"Oh—er!" stammered the young man, "what pleasant weather we are having, aren't we?"

昏暗的灯光、远处传来的音乐声、四周名贵鲜花散发出的花香……这一切的一切正适合求婚。

于是提姆决定试试运气。她很美，这个条件不错，而且，他听说她还是一笔财富的继承人，这个条件更好。

“你不担心有人会为了你的钱而和你结婚吗？”他温柔地问道。

“哦，不担心！我从来没有过这样的念头！”女孩微笑着。

“啊！那么，利萨小姐，”他叹了口气。“你太天真、太单纯了，你做梦也想不到有些男人是多么唯利是图！简直是冷酷无情！”

“也许吧，我没想过。”女孩平静地回答。

“我绝不允许这样可怕的命运降临到你身上。你太好了——太美了！赢得你芳心的那个人，爱的肯定是你这个人。”他说得很热切。

“是的，他也只能如此，”女孩说。“继承那笔钱的是我的堂妹——不是我。你好像把我们两个弄混了。其实我一分钱也没有。”

“哦——呃！”年轻人结巴起来。“今天的天气真不错，是不是？”

(240)

During the period after the university examinations, when an unusually large number of students flunked, one of the boys went to his professor, and said: “I don´t think this is fair, sir; I don´t think I should have a zero on this examination."

"I know it," replied the professor, "but we do not have any mark lower than that."

大学考试结束了，结果异乎寻常，有一大批同学不及格。一个男同学找到教授，对他说："先生，我觉得这不公平。这次考试我不应该得零分。"

"我知道，"教授回答。"可是，我们没有比这更低的分可给了。"

(241)

A certain famous preacher when preaching one Sunday in the summer time observed that many among the congregation ware drowsing. Suddenly, then, he paused, and afterward continued in a loud voice, relating an incident that had no connection whatever with his sermon. This was to the following effect:

"I was once riding along a country road. I came to the house of a farmer, and halted to observe one of the most remarkable sights I have ever seen. There was a sow with a litter of ten little pigs. This sow and each of her offspring had a long curved horn growing out of the forehead between the ears."

The clergyman again paused, and ran his

eye over the congregation. Everybody was now wide-awake. He thereupon remarked:

"Behold how strange! A few minutes since, when I was telling you the truth, you went to sleep. But now when you have heard a whopping lie, you are all wide-awake."

一个夏日的星期天，小有名气的传教士正在布道，他发现许多信众在打盹儿。于是，他突然停顿了一会儿，然后提高嗓门儿，开始给大家讲一件与布道毫无关系的事情：

"有一次，我走在乡村小路上。我来到一家农舍前，停了下来，眼前的景象是我从来也没见过的：有一个母猪带着十个小猪仔，母猪和每个小猪仔两耳之间的额头上都长着一个长长的弯犄角。"

传教士又一次停顿下来，目光扫视着台下，所有的信众现在都瞪大了眼睛在听。于是，他说：

"看看，多奇怪！几分钟前，我在给你们讲真理，你们却昏昏欲睡。现在，你们听到的是弥天大谎，却清醒异常。"

(242)

The juryman petitioned the court to be excused, declaring:

"I owe a man twenty-five dollars that I borrowed, and as he is leaving town to-day for some years I want to catch him before he gets to the train and pay him the money."

"You are excused," the judge announced in a very cold voice. "I don´t want anybody on the jury who can lie like you."

陪审员向法庭请假,他是这样陈述理由的:

"我借了一个人二十五块钱还没还。那个人今天就要到别的地方去,几年之内不会回来。我想赶到火车站,把钱还给他。"

"准许请假。"法官冷冷地宣布。"我不想陪审团里有你这样能撒谎的人。"

(243)

The tender young mother detected her baby boy in a deliberate lie. With tears in her eyes, and a catch in her voice, she sought to impress upon him the enormity of his offense.

"Do you know," she questioned severely, "what happens to little boys who tell falsehoods?"

The culprit shook his head in great distress, and the mother explained carefully:

"Why, a great big black man, with horns on his head and one eye in the center of his forehead, comes along and grabs the little boy who has told a falsehood, and flies with him up to the moon, and keeps him there sifting ashes all the rest of his life. You won´t ever tell another falsehood, will you, darling? It´s wicked!"

Mother´s baby boy regarded the speaker with round-eyed admiration.

"Oh, ma," he gurgled, "what a whopper!"

年轻温柔的母亲发觉她的儿子在故意撒谎。为了让孩子明白撒谎的恶果，她眼里含着泪水，声音哽噎地质问道：

"你知道撒谎的孩子会受到什么惩罚吗？"

犯了错的孩子难过地摇了摇头，于是，妈妈耐心地解释道：

"知道吗？一个头上长着犄角，一只眼睛长在额头上的黑色巨人，会走过来，抓住撒谎的孩子，把他带到月亮上去，让他一辈子都在那里筛灰尘。所以，以后千万不能再撒谎了。好吗，宝贝？撒谎不好！"

孩子睁大了眼睛，崇拜地看着妈妈。

"妈妈，"他咯咯地笑着说："我喜欢您撒的这个谎！"

(244)

"And would you love me as much if father lost all his money?"

"Has he?"

"Why, no."

"Of course I would, darling."

"如果我爸爸没钱了,你还会这样爱我吗?"

"他已经没钱了?"

"哦,没有。"

"当然,亲爱的,我会爱你的。"

(245)

Some physicians direct their patients to lie always on the right side, declaring that it is injurious to the health to lie on both sides. Yet, lawyers as a class enjoy good health.

有些医生叮嘱他们的病人总是靠右侧睡觉,说靠两侧睡会伤身体。可是,律师一族靠两侧睡,身体却很健康。

(注:lie on both sides是个双关语,可以是靠两侧睡,也可以是两边都撒谎的意思。)

（246）

"Are you sure this handbag is genuine crocodile skin?" the woman asked the shopkeeper.

"Absolutely," was the reply. "I shot that crocodile myself."

"But it is badly soiled."

"Well, yes, of course. That´s where it hit the ground, when it fell out of the tree."

"您肯定这个手提包是真鳄鱼皮的吗？"女人问店主。

"千真万确，那条鳄鱼是我亲手打死的。"

"可是，上面有很多土。"

"这个嘛，是这样的，鳄鱼从树上掉下来的时候，这边着地了。"

（247）

Office Boy (anxious to go to football match): "May I have the afternoon off, Sir? My grand—"

Employer: "Oh, yes, I´ve heard that before. Your grandmother died last week."

Office Boy: "Yes, Sir; but—my grandfather´s getting married again this afternoon."

有个想去看足球比赛的年轻人：“先生，下午我可以请一下假吗？我祖……”

老板：“噢，当然，我早就听说了。你的祖母上周去世了。”

年轻人：“是的，先生。可是——我祖父今天下午要再婚。”

（248）

“Yes, dear, I´m going out to−night. I´ve been asked to take supper with an old comrade in arms.”

“By the way, darling, how many men did your regiment muster?”

“亲爱的，今晚我要出去。他们请我去和以前的老战友吃饭。”

“亲爱的，顺便问一句，你们团到底有多少人？”

10. 无言以对

Speechless

(249)

Many a mayor is a friend to the people—just like his honor in the following story.

A taxpayer entered the office of the water registrar in a small city, and explained himself and his business there as follows:

"My name is O'Rafferty. And my cellar is full of water, and my hens will all be drowned entirely if it isn't fixed. And I'm here to inform you that I'm wanting it fixed."

It was explained to the complainant that the remedy for his need must be sought at the office of the mayor, and he therefore departed to interview that official.

After an interval of a few days, O'Rafferty made a second visit to the office of the registrar.

"Sure, and I've come again to tell you that my cellar is now fuller of water than ever it was before. And I'm telling you that I want it fixed, and I'm a man that carries votes in my pocket."

The registrar again explained that he was powerless in the matter, and that the only recourse must be to the mayor.

"The mayor is out!" O´Rafferty snorted. "Sure and didn´t I see the mayor? I did that! And what did the mayor say to me? Huh! he said, ´Mr. O´Rafferty, why don´t you keep ducks?´"

很多市长都以人民为友，就像下面故事里的这位大人。

小城里一位纳税人走进自来水办公室，这样向登记员说明了他的事由：

“我是欧·瑞佛迪。我的地下室被水淹了，如果不及时修理，我养的母鸡都要被淹死了。我来这里就是想要你们去修修。”

对此，他得到的解释是这件事情必须交由市长办公室处理，于是，他又去找市长。

几天之后，欧·瑞佛迪又来到自来水办公室。

“我来是想告诉您我的地下室被水淹了，比以前更厉害了。我来是想让你们去修修。我的口袋里可装着选票呢。”

登记员又一次解释说，对此他无能为力，只能找市长解决。

“市长出去了！”欧·瑞佛迪粗声说道。“再说，你以为我没去找市长吗？我去找了。你知道市长对我说什么吗？哈！他说：‘欧·瑞佛迪，你为什么不养些鸭子呢？’”

(250)

The paying teller told mournfully of his experience with a strange woman who appeared at his wicket to have a check cashed.

"But, madam," he advised her, "you will have to get some one to introduce you before I can pay you the money on this check."

The woman stared at him disdainfully.

"Sir!" she said haughtily. "I wish you to understand that I am here strictly on business. I am not making a social call. I do not care to know you."

银行的付款员不无悲伤地讲起了和一个找他取钱的陌生女人打交道的经过。

当时他对这个女人说:"夫人,你得找一个介绍人,我才能把支票上的钱付给您。"

那个女人轻蔑地盯着他看了一会儿,傲慢地说:"先生,我希望你搞清楚,我来这里是取钱的,可不是来做什么社交拜访。所以无所谓认不认识你。"

(251)

The ice on the river was in perfect condition. A small boy, with his skates on his arm, knocked at the door of the Civil War veteran, who had lost a leg in the war. When the door was opened by the old man, the boy asked:

"Are you going out to-day, sir?"

"Well, no, I guess not, sonny," was the answer. "Why?"

"If you ain´t," the boy suggested, "I thought I might like to borrow your wooden leg to play hockey."

河上结了很厚的冰，正适合滑冰。一个小男孩儿胳膊上搭着他的冰鞋，敲响了内战老兵的房门。那位老兵在战争中失去了一条腿。老人过来开了门，男孩儿问道：

"先生，您今天出去吗？"

"哦，不，我想我不会出去。小家伙，有事吗？"

"如果不出去，"男孩儿提议道，"我想借你的木头腿去玩曲棍球。"

（252）

A traveler in the South chatted with an aged negro, whom he met in the road.

"And I suppose you were once a slave?" he remarked.

"Yes, sir," the old colored man

answered.

"And, so, after the war, you gained your freedom," the gentleman continued.

But the ancient one shook his head sadly.

"No, sir," he declared with great emphasis. "Not exactly, sir. I didn't get my freedom, sir, after de war—I got married!"

一个来南方旅游的人在路上遇到一个上了年纪的黑人，他们闲谈起来。

游人问："你以前是奴隶吧？"

"没错，先生，"老人回答。

"后来，内战结束，你获得了自由。"游人继续说道。

"没有，先生，"他强调说，"不完全是，其实战后我没有获得自由——因为我结婚了。"

(253)

The applicant for the position of cook explained to the lady why she had left her last place:

"To tell the truth, mum, I just couldn't stand the way the master and the mistress was always quarreling."

"That must have been unpleasant," the lady agreed.

"Yes, mum," the cook declared, "they

was at it all the time. When it wasn′t me an′ him, it was me an′ her."

前来应聘厨师的女人向新女主人解释她离开上一家主人的原因：

"告诉您实话，夫人，那家的男主人和女主人总在争吵，我实在无法忍受。"

"那肯定让人很不愉快，"女士表示理解。

"是呀，他们总在吵。如果我不和男主人吵，就会和女主人吵。"

(254)

The physician advised his patient to eat a hearty dinner at night, without any worry over the ability to digest it. The patient, however, protested:

"But the other time when I came to see you, you insisted I must eat only a very light supper in the evening."

The physician nodded, smiling complacently.

"Yes, of course—that shows what great progress the science of medicine is making."

医生建议他的病人晚上要饱餐一顿，不要担心消化问题。病人很疑惑地问：

"可是上次我来看病,你嘱咐我晚餐一定要少吃。"

医生点点头,得意地微笑着说:

"没错,这表明医学现在取得了很大的进步。"

(255)

The customer asked for fresh eggs, and the clerk in the

Shopper:— "Are these eggs fresh?"

Apprentice:— "Yes, ma´am, they be."

Shopper:— "How long since they were laid?"

Apprentice:— "´Tain´t ten minutes, ma´am—I know, I laid them eggs there myself."

顾客:"这些鸡蛋新鲜吗?"

学徒:"新鲜,夫人。"

顾客:"这些鸡蛋下了多长时间了?"

学徒:"还不到十分钟,夫人,我很清楚,因为是我下(放在这里)的。"

(注:此处,laid 意为下蛋,还可以是放置的意思。)

(256)

It was a rule of the club that anyone asking a question which he himself could not answer must pay a fine. One of the members presented a question as to why a ground-squirrel in digging left no dirt around the entrance to its hole. He was finally called on for the answer, and explained that of course the squirrel began at the bottom and dug upward.

"Excellent!" a listener laughed. "But how does the squirrel manage to reach the bottom?"

"That," said the other with a grin, "is your question."

俱乐部规定，如果谁问了一个连他自己都回答不上来的问题的话，就必须受罚。有一位会员的问题是为什么黄鼠挖洞时，洞口周围没有积土。没人能回答他的问题，于是，最后由他来回答。他解释说当然是因为黄鼠是从坑底开始往上挖的。

"没错！"一个听众笑道。"但是，黄鼠是怎样到坑底的呢？"

刚才出题的人坏笑着说："这算是你的问题了。"

(257)

Amos Perkins was hired in the spring to shoot muskrats, which were overrunning the mill dam. An acquaintance paused to chat one day with Amos, who was sitting at ease on the bank of the stream, his gun safely out of reach.

"I hear the muskrats are undermining the dam," the acquaintance said.

"So they be, so they be!" Amos agreed.

"Hi! there goes one!" cried the visitor, pointing. "Shoot! Why don´t you shoot, man?"

Amos spat tobacco juice emphatically, and answered: "Huh! think I want to lose my job?"

春天，阿摩司受雇射杀水坝上泛滥成灾的麝鼠。一天，一个熟人路过水坝，便停下来和他聊天，当时，阿摩司悠然自得地坐在河岸边，猎枪安然地远远放在一边。

“我听说麝鼠在破坏大坝，”熟人说。

“是的，没错。”阿摩司回答。

“喂，瞧，那边就有一个！”熟人喊道。“快打！喂，你怎么不打呢？”

阿摩司狠狠地将口中的烟叶吐出来，回答说：“你想让我以后没差事干不成？”

(258)

Back in those days when corporal punishment was permitted to teachers, a minor teacher named Miss Bings complained to one of her superiors, Miss Manners, that she had spanked one particular boy, Thomas, until she could spank him no more for physical fatigue.

"When you want him spanked again, send him to me," Miss Manners said.

Next morning, Thomas came into the presence of Miss Manners, displaying an air that was downcast. The teacher regarded him with suspicion.

"Did you come from Miss Bings?" she asked sharply.

"Yes, ma´am," Thomas admitted.

"I thought as much!" On the instant, she skillfully inverted the youngster over her lap, and whacked him in a most spirited manner. This duty done, as the wailings of the boy died away, she demanded sternly:

"And now what have you to say?"

"Please, ma´am," Thomas answered brokenly, "Miss Bings wants the scissors!"

以前，还允许老师体罚学生的时候，有一个叫宾斯小姐的年轻老师对她的领导迈纳斯小姐抱怨说，她打了一个叫托马斯的学生的屁股，结果到后来，她实在太累，打不动了。

“以后你要是想打他屁股，就把他送到我这里来。”迈纳斯小姐说。

第二天早晨，托马斯无精打采地来到迈纳斯小姐面前。迈纳斯小姐上下打量着他，目光锐利地问道：

“是宾斯小姐叫你来的吗？”

“是的，夫人。”托马斯承认。

“我说呢！”话音刚落，她就轻车熟路地把小男孩放倒在她的大腿上，狠狠地打了几下。然后，等男孩的哭声小了点儿的时候，她厉声问道：

“这下，你还有什么可说的？”

“夫人，”托马斯抽抽搭搭地说，“宾斯小姐让我来拿剪刀。”

(259)

A tramp devised a new scheme for working on the sympathy of the housewife. After ringing the front door bell, he got on his knees, and began nibbling at the grass of the lawn. Presently the woman opened the door, and, in surprise at sight of him on all fours, asked what he was doing there.

The tramp got to his feet shakily, and made an eloquent clutch at his stomach as he explained:

“Dear madam, I am so hungry that I just had to take to eatin´ grass.”

“Well, well, now ain´t that too bad!” the woman cried. “You go right into the back yard—the grass there is longer."

一个流浪汉想出了一条锦囊妙计来博得一位主妇的同情。他先摁了一下门铃，然后，赶紧跪在草坪上，开始啃草。很快，女主人开了门，看到流浪汉匍匐在那里，很吃惊地问他在那里干什么。

流浪汉颤颤巍巍地站起来，装出一副痛苦的样子捂着肚子说：

"亲爱的夫人，我太饿了，所以，只好吃草充饥。"

"这样呀，太可怜了！"女主人说。"那你去后边院子里吧，那里的草比较长。"

(260)

During an exciting game of football a player had two fingers of his right hand badly smashed, and on his way home from the ground he dropped into the doctor's to have them attended to.

"Doctor," he asked, anxiously. "When this hand of mine heals, will I be able to play the piano?"

"Certainly you will," the doctor assured him.

"Then you're a wonder, doctor. I never could before."

激烈的足球赛中，一位球员的右手两个手指不幸骨折了，回家的路上，他顺便去看医生。

“医生，”他焦虑地问，“您说，我的手好之后，能弹钢琴吗？”

“当然能了。”医生安慰他说。

“您简直就是神医。我以前可不会弹钢琴。”

(261)

“Are all flowers popular?” asked the teacher.

“No, ma´am,” replied one of the bright little girls.

“What flowers are not popular?”

“Wall-flowers, ma´am.”

老师问：“是不是所有的花都受欢迎？”

“不是，夫人，”一个聪明伶俐的小女孩儿回答。

“那么什么花不受欢迎呢？”

“墙花。”

（注：舞会上，坐在墙边没有舞伴的女孩被称作“墙花”。）

(262)

A small boy was playing with an iron hoop in the street, when suddenly it bounced through the railings and broke the kitchen window of one of the areas. The lady of the house waited with anger in her eyes for the appearance of the hoop´s owner. He arrived.

"Please, I´ve broken your window," he said, "and father´s come to mend it."

Sure enough the boy was followed by a man, who at once set to work, while the boy, taking his hoop, ran off. The window finished, the man said:

"That´ll be three shillings, mum."

"Three shillings!" gasped the woman. "But your son broke it. The little fellow with the hoop. You´re his father, aren´t you?"

The man shook his head.

"Never seen him before," he said. "He came round to my place and said his mother wanted her window mended. You´re his mother, aren´t you?"

And the good woman could only shake her head; for once words failed her.

有个小男孩儿在街上玩铁环，突然，铁环越过栏杆，打碎了小区里一扇厨房的玻璃窗。房子的女主人眼里冒着怒火，等待着铁环主人的出现。

"对不起，我打碎了您的窗户，"小男孩儿说，"我爸爸来给您修理了。"

的确，那个男孩儿的身后跟着一个男人，这个

男人很快投入了工作。而小男孩儿则拿起他的铁环,跑了。窗户修好了,男人说:

“请付三先令,夫人。”

“三先令!”女人张大了嘴,“可是,窗户是您儿子打碎的,就是那个拿铁环的小孩儿。您不是他的父亲吗?”

男人摇摇头。

“从来没见过他,他跑过来找我,说他妈妈想找人修窗户。您不是他妈妈吗?”

傻傻的女人只能摇头叹息,一时间,说不出话来。

(263)

During a conversation between an Irishman and a Jew, the Irishman asked how it was that the Jews were so wise.

“Because,” said the Jew, “we eat a certain kind of fish;” and he offered to sell one for ten dollars.

After paying his money, the Irishman received a small dried fish. He bit into it, then exclaimed: “Why, this is only a smoked herring.”

“See?” said the Jew. “You are getting wise already.”

一个爱尔兰人和一个犹太人聊天时,爱尔兰

人问为什么犹太人这么聪明。

"因为，"犹太人回答，"我们吃一种鱼。"然后他提出可以10美元卖给他一条。

付完钱之后，爱尔兰人得到了一条小干鱼。他咬了一口，然后大叫起来：

"喂，这只不过是条熏青鱼。"

"明白了吧？" 犹太人说，"你现在也变聪明了。"

（264）

"Yes," said the old man to his visitor, "I am proud of my girls and would like to see them comfortably married, and as I have made a little money they will not go penniless to their husbands. There is Mary, twenty-five years old, and a really good girl. I shall give her $1000 when she marries. Then comes Bet, who won't see thirty-five again. I shall give her $3000, and the man who takes Eliza, who is forty, will have $5000 with her." The young man reflected a moment and then asked, "You haven't one about fifty, have you?"

老人对客人说："我为我的女儿们感到骄傲，我要看着她们好好地嫁人。我已经小有积蓄，所以，不会让她们身无分文地随丈夫而去。这是玛丽，二十五岁，她可是一个好女孩儿，她结婚的时候我会给她 1000 美元。这是贝蒂，三十五岁，我要给她 3000 美元。如果哪个男人愿意娶伊丽莎白，哦，她四十岁了，我会给他 5000 美元。”年轻人想了想，问道：“您有没有年约五十的女儿呢？”

（265）

The newly married pair quarreled seriously, so that the wife in a passion finally declared:

“I´m going home to my mother!”

The husband maintained his calm in the face of this calamity, and drew out his pocketbook.

“Here,” he said, counting out some bills, “is the money for your railroad fare.”

The wife took it, and counted it in her turn. Then she faced her husband scornfully:

“But that isn´t enough for a return ticket.”

一对新婚夫妇大吵了起来，新娘一气之下大声宣布：

“我要回娘家！”

新郎临危不乱，他从钱包里拿出几张钞票说，“给，这是你买火车票的钱。”

新娘接过钱，数了数，然后直视着新郎，不屑地说：

“这些钱不够买回来的车票。”

(266)

The slow suitor asked:

"Elizabeth, would you like to have a puppy?"

"Oh, Edward," the girl gushed, "how delightfully humble of you. Yes, dearest, I accept."

一个呆头呆脑的小伙子是这样求婚的：

"伊丽莎白，你想不想要一只小狗？"

"噢，埃德华，"女孩儿兴奋地说，"你傻乎乎的样子真让人喜欢，是的，亲爱的，我接受你的求婚。"

(267)

"Well, Ikey, my boy," said Sol to his son, "I´ve made my will and left it all to you."

"That´s very good of you, father," remarked Ike, eyeing him suspiciously. "But, bless you, it cost a lot of money for the lawyer and fees and things!"

"well, it isn´t fair I should pay all that, is it? So I´ll take it off from your next month´s salary."

"艾克，我亲爱的儿子，"索尔对自己的儿子说，"我已经准备好了遗嘱，把所有的财产都留给你了。"

“太感谢了，父亲，”艾克有点不相信地看着他爸爸，“可是，我的好爸爸，请律师，遗嘱费还有其他费用，要花很多钱呢！”

“是的，让我承担这些费用是有点儿不太公平。所以，我决定从你下个月的工资里扣除。”

（268）

Small Boy： “Daddy， here's a ball for you.”

Father: “Where did you get that from?”

Small Boy: “It's a lost ball, Daddy.”

Father: “Are you sure it's a lost ball?”

Small Boy: “Yes, Daddy; they're still looking for it.”

小男孩儿：“爸爸，给你球。”

父亲：“哪来的？”

小男孩儿：“别人丢的。”

父亲：“你怎么知道是别人丢的？”

小男孩儿：“因为他们还在找它。”

（269）

He: “But if you will allow me to—”

She: "Oh! I know what you are going to say, but you're quite mistaken and I can prove it."

他和她正在争吵：

他："你能不能让我把话——"

她："行了，我知道你要说什么，不过你肯定错了，我可以证明。"

(270)

"Well! we've missed that confounded train. What time will the next one be here?"

"If the engine doesn't break down, and the track doesn't spread, and they don't run into any cows, and the up-freight isn't behind time, and the swing bridge isn't open, it ought to be here in about two hours."

"唉！我们没赶上那趟该死的火车。下一趟火车几点到？"

"如果发动机不坏，铁轨不错位，火车不撞上母牛，装车不耽误时间，吊桥不塌，应该在两小时后到达这里。"

(271)

Miss Hen: "I demand an explanation! You told me that your name was plain ´Mr. Rooster,´ and that poet just now addressed you as ´Chanticleer´!"

母鸡小姐："我要讨个说法！你告诉我说你的名字很普通，叫'公鸡先生'，可是刚才那个诗人却称你作'雄鸡'！"

(272)

The burly man spoke lucidly to his gangling adversary:

"You´re a nincompoop, a liar and hoss-thief."

The other man protested, with a whine in his voice:

"Such talk isn´t nice—and, anyhow, ´that isn´t fair twitting´ on facts."

一个壮汉毫不隐讳地对他骨瘦如柴的对手说：

"你是个傻瓜，满嘴谎话，而且偷窃成性。"

对方不无委屈地抗议道：

"这样说话可不好——事实虽然如此，可是你也不能嘲笑，这不公平。"

(273)

"It appears to be your record, Mary," said the magistrate, "that you have already been convicted thirty-five times of stealing."

"I guess that's right, your honor," answered Mary. "No woman is perfect."

地方长官说："玛丽，从记录上看，你已经因为偷窃而被定罪三十五次了。"

"应该没错，"玛丽回答说，"世上没有完美的女人嘛。"

(274)

He: "Crowded, were you? I thought you went early to avoid the rush."

She: "So I did; but about five thousand other people did the same thing."

他："交通拥挤？是吗？我以为你会避开高峰期，提前出门。"

她："我是这样做的，可是大约有五千多人也和我一样提前出门了。"

(275)

Salesman: "Another advantage of this machine, madam, is that it is fool-proof."

Woman (placidly): "No doubt, to the ordinary kind. But you don´t know my husband."

售货员:"太太,这台机器还有另外一个优点,就是傻瓜都能用。"

女士(温和地):"对一般的傻瓜来说肯定不是什么难事,但对我丈夫就不行了。"

(276)

Mother: It is rude to whisper, Humphrey.

Humphrey (aged five): Well, I was saying what a funny nose that man´s got. So you see it would have been much ruder if I´d said it aloud.

妈妈:"汉弗莱,窃窃私语是不礼貌的表现。"

汉弗莱(5岁):"我说的是那个男人的鼻子真可笑!所以,你看如果我大声说会更加不礼貌的。"

(277)

She (pouting): You don´t value my kisses as you used to.

He: Value them? Why, before we were married I used to expect a dozen in payment for a box of candy, and now I consider only one of them sufficient payment for a new dress.

她（板着脸）:“我的吻在你那里已经贬值了。”

他:“贬值？你想想看，结婚前，给你买一盒糖我可以得到十几个亲吻，可是，现在，买一件连衣裙也只能得到一个吻了。”

(278)

“The man that argues with a woman is a fool,” said Mr. Gadspur.

“I agree with you,” said Mr. Twobble.

“And if he expects to have the last word he´s an even bigger fool.”

“Quite so, quite so. What did you and the Missus quarrel about this morning?”

“跟女人辩论的男人都是傻瓜，”盖德斯伯先生说。

“我赞同你的观点。” 陶伯先生说。

"如果他想强辩到底就更傻！"

"的确是这样。那么今天早上你跟太太辩论什么呢？"

(279)

Magistrate: "Can´t this case be settled out of court?"

Mulligan: "Sure, sure; that´s what we were trying to do, your honor, when the police interfered."

法官:"这个案子不能庭外和解吗？"

爱尔兰人:"当然可以。可是我们正试图和解的时候,警察却过来横插了一杠。"

(280)

A candidate for Congress from a certain Western state was never shy about telling the voters why they should send him to Washington. "I am a practical farmer," he said, boastfully, at one meeting. "I can plow, reap, milk cows, shoe a horse—in fact, I should like you to tell me one thing about a farm which I can not do." Then, in the impressive silence, a voice asked from the back of the hall: "Can you lay an egg?"

有一个来自西部某州的人竞选议员。在向那些选民说明为什么他们应该把他选到华盛顿从政的时候,他从来都没有不好意思。在一次选举会上他自夸道:"我是一个很实干的农夫,我会耕田、会收割、会挤牛奶、会给马钉蹄铁……现在,我宁愿你们说出一件我不会干的农活。"一阵鸦雀无声之后,从大厅后面传来一个声音:"你会下蛋吗?"

11. 张冠李戴

Misunderstanding!

(281)

Some persons are born to have honor thrust upon them, and such is obviously the case of the actor named in this story.

The colored maid of an actress took out for exercise her mistress´s dog, a splendid St. Bernard. A passer-by admired the animal, and inquired as to the breed. The maid said:

"I doan jes´ zactly know mahself, but I dun hear my missis say he am a full-blood Sam Bernard."

有些人天生就好运当头。本故事中的男演员显然就是这样的一个人。

一位女佣替女演员外出遛狗。这是一条非常棒的圣伯纳德犬。有位过路者对此狗称羡不已，并询问狗的品种。该女佣回答：

"我不是很清楚，不过，我听我的女主人说这条狗是纯种的萨姆伯纳德。"

（注：St.Bernard 是一种有名的工作犬，而 Sam Bernard 是英国著名的电影演员，此处，女佣错把前者记成了后者，从而闹出了天大的笑话。）

(282)

The editor of a country newspaper betook himself to a party at the house of a neighbor, where, only a few weeks earlier, a baby had been added to the family. On the editor´s arrival at the house, he was met at the door by his hostess, a woman who suffered to some extent from deafness. After the usual exchange of greetings, the editor inquired concerning the health of the baby. The hostess had a severe cold, and she now misunderstood the visitor´s inquiry concerning the baby, thinking that he was solicitous on her account. So she explained to the aghast editor who had asked about the baby that, although she usually had one every winter, this was the very worst one she had ever had, it kept her awake at night a great deal, and at first confined her to her bed. Having explained thus far, the good lady noticed the flabbergasted air of her guest. She continued sympathetically; saying that she could tell by his looks and the way he acted that he was going to have one just like hers. Then she insisted that, as a precautionary measure for the sake of his condition, he should come in out of the draft and sit down and stay quiet.

有一家乡村小报的编辑来邻居家做客，这家邻居几周前刚刚喜降一个婴儿。编辑来到邻居家门口的时候，出来迎接的是女主人，这个女人有点耳聋。寒暄问候之后，编辑询问孩子的健康状况。

女主人刚好得了感冒，所以，她误解了编辑的话，以为他询问的是她自己的感冒状况，于是，她对编辑解释说：一般情况下，每年冬天都得得一次，这次是最严重的一次，让她晚上无法入睡，而且刚开始，必须卧床休息。说到这里，她发现客人神色不对，于是，安慰说，看他的神色，她觉得他也要和她一样得一次。于是，她坚持让他进屋，坐下休息一会儿，以便提前预防。

（注：女主人说的是感冒，而编辑则以为她说的是生孩子。）

（283）

A popular Oklahoma City salesman recently married, and was accompanied by his wife as he entered the dining-room of a Texas hotel famed for its excellent cuisine. His order was served promptly, but the fried chicken he had been telling his wife so much about was not in evidence.

"Where is my chicken?" he asked somewhat irritably.

The dusky waiter, leaning over and bringing his mouth in close proximity to the salesman's ear, replied:

"If you mean the little girl with blue eyes and fluffy hair, she doesn't work here any more."

一个很受大家欢迎的俄克拉荷马市的推销员最近结婚了。他在妻子的陪伴下，来到了德克萨斯州一家饭店的餐厅。这家餐厅的厨艺非常有名。他点的菜很快就上来了，但是，他曾对妻子赞不绝口的炸鸡却迟迟不见踪影。

“我的鸡呢？”他有点不耐烦地质问道。

长得有点黑的男服务生，靠近他，把嘴巴贴近他的耳朵，说：

“你是说那个蓝眼睛，披着长发的小妞吗？她已经不在这里干了。”

(284)

"I say, Madge, it´s bitterly cold. Hadn´t you better put something on your chest?"

"Don´t worry, old thing. I´ve powdered it three times."

“喂，我说玛琪，天很冷。你最好在身上盖点东西。”

“别担心，老头子。我已经抹了三次粉了。”

(285)

Gushing Lady: "Yes, she´s married to a lawyer, and a good honest fellow too."

Cynic: "Bigamist!"

快言快语的女士："她嫁给了一个律师，也嫁给了一个诚实的好小伙儿。"

喜欢鸡蛋里挑骨头的人："可这是重婚啊！"

(286)

The instructor in the Medical College exhibited a diagram.

"The subject here limps," he explained, "because one leg is shorter than the other." He addressed one of the students:

"Now, Mr. Snead, what would you do in such a case?"

Young Snead pondered earnestly and replied with conviction:

"I fancy, sir, that I should limp, too."

医学院的老师正在解释一副人体挂图：

"看，这个病人是个瘸子，因为他的一条腿短，另一条腿长。"

他问其中一个学生：

"请问，斯尼德同学，在这种情况下你会怎么做呢？"

年轻的斯尼德认真地想了想，坚定地答道：

“我想，我也会瘸的。”

（注：英语中case的意思可以是“病例”，也可以理解为“在……情况下”，此处，老师问的是针对该病例学生怎么处理，显然学生误解了老师的意思。）

（287）

On her return home after an absence of a few hours, the mother was displeased to find that little Emma, who was ailing, had not taken her pill at the appointed time, although she had been carefully directed to do so.

“You were very naughty, Emma,” the mother chided. “I told you to be sure and take that pill.”

“But, mamma,” the child pleaded in extenuation, “you didn´t tell me where to take it to.”

离家几小时之后，妈妈回到家里，她发现生病的小艾玛没有照她的叮嘱按时吃药。

“艾玛，你真不听话，”妈妈责备道：“我不是告诉过你要take(吃)药吗？”

“可是，妈妈，”孩子无辜地申辩道：“你没有告诉我应该把药take(拿)到哪里去。”

（注：英文中的吃药要用动词take，而take的另外一个最常用的意思是“拿，带”。）

(288)

"Did your watch stop when it dropped on the floor?" asked one man of his friend.

"Sure," was the answer. "Did you think it would go through?"

"你的手表掉在地上之后没停吗？"他的一个朋友问。

"当然停了。"他回答，"你以为它能掉到地底下去吗？"

(289)

Just before the service the clergyman was called into the vestibule by a young couple, who asked that he should marry them. He answered he had not time then, but that if they would wait until after the sermon he would be glad to do so. Accordingly, just before the end of the service, he announced:

"Will those who wish to be married today please come forward?"

Thirteen women and one man quickly stepped up.

神父刚要主持礼拜，一对年轻人就把他叫到走廊里，请他为他们主持婚礼。神父说现在没时间，如果愿意，可以等到布道结束之后，那时他会很乐意为他们主持婚礼。因此，在礼拜结束的时候，他如约大声问道："今天想结婚的人，请到前面来吧！"

话音未落，就有十三个女人和一个男人走向前来。

(290)

Nurse: "You were very naughty in church, Guy. Do you know where little boys and girls go to who don't put their pennies in the collection box?"

Guy: "Yes, nurse; to the pictures."

保姆："小家伙，你们在教堂里太淘气了。你们知道那些不把零钱投进募捐箱里的孩子们会去哪里吗？"

小家伙："知道，阿姨，他们去看电影了。"

(291)

The passing lady mistakenly supposed that the woman shouting from a window down the street was calling to the little girl minding baby brother close by on the curb.

"Your mother is calling you," she said kindly.

The little girl corrected the lady:

"She isn´t calling we. Us don´t belong to she."

一位女士路过街边的一个窗口，窗口那儿有个女人正在朝街头喊话，女士以为她是在喊街头照顾小弟弟的女孩儿，于是便善意地提醒道：

"你们的妈妈在叫你们呢。"

小女孩儿纠正道：

"她叫的不是我们，我们不是她家的。"

（292）

The teacher asked the little girl if she was going to the Maypole dance. "No, I ain´t going," was the reply.

The teacher corrected the child:

"You must not say, ´I ain´t going,´ you must say, ´I am not going.´" And she added to impress the point: "I am not going. He is not going. We are not going. You are not going. They are not going. Now, dear, can you say all that?"

The little girl nodded and smiled brightly.

"Sure!" she replied. "They aren´t

nobody going."

老师问小女孩，她是不是要去参加五朔节舞会。小女孩儿回答："不,I aren't going.(我不去。)"

老师纠正道：

"你不能说 I aren't going,你应该说，I am not going."然后，为了说得更明白，她补充道："I am not going. He is not going. We are not going. You are not going. They are not going. 现在，亲爱的，你会说了吗？"

小女孩儿点点头，露出灿烂的笑容。

"会了！"她回答。"They aren't nobody going."

(293)

Prison Visitor: "Am I right in presuming that it was your passion for strong drink that brought you here?"

Prisoner: "I don't think you can know this place, governor. It's the last place on earth I'd come to if I was looking for anything to drink."

监狱视察官："你到这里来是因为嗜酒如命，对吗？"

囚犯："长官，我想你还不了解这个地方。如果我想喝什么的话，最不能来的地方就是这里。"

12. 自作聪明

Too Smart

(294)

One Japanese bragged to another that he made a fan last twenty years by opening only a fourth section, and using this for five years, then the next section, and so on.

The other Japanese registered scorn.

"Wasteful!" he ejaculated. "I was better taught. I make a fan last a lifetime. I open it wide, and hold it under my nose quite motionless. Then I wave my head."

有一个日本人对另外一个日本人吹嘘说他的扇子用了二十年，但才打开了四分之一，这四分之一他还打算再用上五年，然后才打开下一个四分之一，如此节省地用下去。

另外一个日本人表现出明显的不屑：

"太浪费了！"他迫不及待地嚷嚷道，"我可比你在行多了，我的扇子能用一辈子。我把扇子完全打开，放在我的鼻子底下纹丝不动，然后，我摇动我的头。"

(295)

Jim: "That McCormack is heavy - weight—my cousin used to go to school with him."

Billie: "That is nothing.—My brother had three front teeth knocked out by him once."

吉姆:"那个麦考马克块头好大——我堂哥以前总是和他一起去上学。"

比利:"那有什么了不起的——有一次，我哥哥的三个门牙就是他打掉的。"

(296)

Father: "Well, son, you certainly made a fool of yourself! That girl robbed you of every cent you had."

Son: "Well, dad, you have to hand it to me for picking them clever."

父亲:"儿子,这次你丢人丢到家了!那个女孩骗走了你身上所有的钱。"

儿子:"不过,老爹,你得佩服我弄到这些钱的手段还算高明。"

(297)

A man entered a jeweler's in Liverpool and asked to be shown some "very good watches." The proprietor, a Jew, being absent, the prospective customer was attended to by his daughter, who got out three watches, marked respectively £5, £4, and £3 , and laid them in a row on the counter.

The man, after looking very closely at them, called the attention of the Jewess to a watch on a shelf behind her; as she turned to obtain the watch he placed the higher-priced watch, in the place of the lower-priced one, and, not caring for the watch now shown him, said: "Me no like that; I take cheaper watch," paid £3 , and departed.

Soon the girl discovered the deception, and told her father on his return.

"Never mind, my dear," said he, with a smile; "dose watches cost all de same price—two pound."

有一个人走进了利物浦的一家珠宝店，他要看看“最好的手表”。店老板是个犹太人，当时刚好不在店里，所以，他的小女儿出来接待这个顾客。她拿出三只手表摆在柜台上，上面标价依次为5 英镑、4 英镑和 3 英镑。

这个人很仔细地查看了一会儿，然后指小女孩儿背后架子上的一个手表要看，就在小女孩儿转身去拿那个手表之际，他把标价贵的手表和便宜的手表调了一下位置。然后，他看也没看刚刚拿来的手表，说："我不喜欢这个手表，我还是买这个便宜的吧。"于是，付了三美元之后，他就离开了。

很快，小女孩儿发现了骗局。爸爸回来后，她把这件事告诉了他。

"没关系，亲爱的，"爸爸笑着说，"那些手表其实都是一个价，都卖两美元。"

（298）

An airman had been taking up passengers for short trips, and by the time his last trip came was absolutely fed up by being asked silly questions. He told his passengers, two ladies, that on no account were they to speak to him; that he could not talk and give his attention to his machine, and that they must keep silent. Up they went, and the airman quite enjoyed himself. He looped the looped and practiced all sorts of stunts to his own satisfaction with no interruption from his passengers until he felt a touch on his arm. "What is it?" he said impatiently. "I´m so sorry to trouble you," said a voice behind, "and I know I oughtn´t to speak. I do apologize sincerely, but I can´t help it. I thought perhaps you ought to know Annie´s gone."

一个带乘客进行短途飞行的飞行员，在最后一次飞行的时候，已经彻底厌倦了乘客提出的那些愚蠢的问题，于是，他叮嘱两名乘客（这次是两个女的）千万不要跟他讲话，他说，他不能说话，要全神贯注地开飞机，所以她们必须保持沉默。这次他开得很开心，在空中转了一圈又一圈，还做了各种特技动作。正在他因为没有乘客打扰而心满意足的时候，感到有人在拍他的肩膀。“什么事？”他不耐烦地问。“我很抱歉打扰你，”身后的人说，“我知道我不应该说话。实在很抱歉，但我不能不说了。我想也许你应该知道，安妮不见了。”

（299）

Boss: What do you mean by such language? Are you the manager here or am I?

Jones: I know I´m not the manager.

The Boss: Very well, then, if you´re not the manager, why do you talk like a blamed idiot?

老板：你这样说话是什么意思？你是这里的经理，还是我是这里的经理？

琼斯：我知道我不是经理。

老板：很好，那么，如果你不是经理，为什么你说话像个该死的白痴？

(300)

The breakfaster in the cheap restaurant tried to make conversation with the man beside him at the counter.

"Awful rainy spell—like the flood."

"The flood?" The tone was polite, but inquiring.

"The flood—Noah, the Ark, Mount Ararat."

The other bit off half a slice of bread, shook his head, and mumbled thickly:

"Haven´t read today´s paper yet."

在一家廉价餐馆，正在吃早餐的一位食客与他身边的另一位食客搭讪道：

"雨下得可真大——有点像那场洪水。"

"那场洪水？"对方很礼貌，但有点迷惑。

"就是那场洪水——诺亚，方舟，还有阿勒山。"

对方咬了一片面包，摇了摇头，粗声粗气地咕哝道：

"我还没读今天的报纸呢。"

(301)

"What is the use of quarreling, my dear girl? Let us forgive and forget."

"That is just the trouble. I am always

forgiving, and you are always forgetting."

"亲爱的，争吵有什么用呢？让我们相互原谅并且忘记这一切吧。"

"问题就在这儿。我总在原谅，而你总在忘记。"

(302)

"Ever get any nice butter?" queried old Grumpy.

"Supply in every day," replied his provision merchant suavely.

"Then why in thunder don't you sell it?" asked Grumpy.

"你们有好黄油吗？"坏脾气的老人质问道。

"每天都有。"供应商温和地回答。

"那为什么不卖？"

(303)

Two men met on the city street in the evening, and had a number of drinks together. The one who lived in the suburbs became confidential, and exhibited a string tied around a finger.

"I don't dare to go home," he explained. "There's something my wife told me to do, without fail, and to make sure I wouldn't forget, she tied that string around my finger. But for the life of me I can't remember what the thing was I am to do. And I don't dare to go home!"

A few days later the two men met again, this time in the afternoon.

"Well," the one asked, "did you finally remember what that string was to remind you of?"

The other showed great gloom in his expression, as he replied:

"I didn't go home until the next night, just because I was scared, and then my wife told me what the string was for all right—she certainly did!" There was a note of pain in his voice. "The string was to remind me to be sure to come home early."

一天晚上，两个朋友在城里的街上相遇，就在一起喝了几杯。几杯酒下肚，那个住在郊区的人开始向朋友掏心窝。他伸出手，让朋友看他手指上缠着的细绳子。

"我现在不敢回家，"他说，"我老婆交代给我的任务，让我必须做到，不要忘了，为了提醒我，她在我的手指上系了这个细绳子。可是，我怎么也想不起来我老婆交代给我的是什么事情。所以，不敢回家了！"

几天之后，两个朋友又见面了，这次是在午后。

朋友问道:“上次，你想起来那个细绳子是提醒你干什么的了吗？”

另一位极其伤心地回答说：

“那天,我很害怕,所以第二天晚上才敢回家。可是,回家之后,我老婆告诉我那个细绳子是平安绳——她的确很担心我!”男人充满了痛苦地继续说道:“那个绳子是提醒我早点儿回家的。”

(304)

The traveling salesman instructed the porter that he must leave the train at Cleveland, where he was due at three o´clock in the morning. He explained that violence might be necessary because he did not wake easily. He emphasized his instructions with a generous tip.

The drummer awoke at six in the morning, with Cleveland far behind. In a rage, he sought the porter. The colored man was in a highly disheveled state and his face was bruised badly. His eyes popped at sight of the furious traveling man, who allowed no opportunity for explanations or excuses. He did all the talking, and did it forcibly. When at last the outraged salesman went away, the porter shook his head dismally, and muttered:

"Now, I should wonder whom I had put off at Cleveland."

乘火车旅行的推销员告诉乘务员，说他凌晨三点必须在克里夫兰下车。他让乘务员无论如何也要叫醒他，哪怕采取暴力都行，因为他睡觉比较死。为此，他还给了乘务员一笔可观的小费。

推销员早晨六点钟醒来，发现克里夫兰早过了。盛怒之下，他找到乘务员。那个黑人乘务员头发凌乱，脸上还留着伤痕。看到怒气冲天的推销员，他不由得睁大了眼睛。可是，推销员根本不容他解释，只自顾自地发泄着心中的怒气。最后，愤怒的推销员走了，乘务员黯然地摇了摇头，咕哝道：

"奇怪，在克里夫兰我把谁扔下车了呢？"

(305)

Dob: "What's that piece of cord tied around your finger for?"

Botham: "My wife put it there to remind me to post her letter."

"And did you post it?"

"No; she forgot to give it to me!"

岛伯："你手指上为什么缠着绳子？"

伯塞姆："是我妻子缠的，想提醒我帮她寄信。"

"那么你寄了吗？"

"没有，她忘了把信给我。"

（306）

"Rather absent-minded, isn't he?"

"Extremely so. Why, the other night when he got home he knew there was something he wanted to do, but he couldn't remember what it was until he had sat up over an hour trying to think."

"And did he finally remember it?"

"Yes, he discovered that he wanted to go to bed early."

"他有点儿健忘，是不是？"

"千真万确！那天晚上，他回到家，知道有件事情要做，可是就是想不起来了。他坐在那里想呀想呀，想了一个小时。"

"最后他想起来了吗？"

"想起来了。他想做的事情是早点儿睡觉。"

(307)

"I know I´m old, but I´m crazy about you," stated Mr. Moneybags. "When I go I´ll leave all my fortune to you if you´ll have me."

"Have you any bad habits?" asked Miss Goldielocks, thoughtfully.

"Only that I walk in my sleep, if you could call that a bad habit."

"You dear old thing. Of course I´ll marry you. And we´ll have our honeymoon on the top floor of some tall hotel, won´t we?"

富翁先生说:"我知道我老了,但是我爱你。如果你接受我，我死后就把我所有的财产都留给你。"

金发小姐若有所思地问:"那你有什么不良习惯吗？"

"我梦游,如果这也算是不良习惯的话。"

"亲爱的老家伙。当然我会嫁给你。我们的蜜月安排在某个高层饭店的顶楼,好不好？"

13. 异想天开
How Can It Happen?

(308)

"Do you really believe in heredity?"

"Most certainly I do. That is how I came into all my money."

"你相信遗传吗？"

"当然相信了。我所有的钱都是这么来的。"

(309)

Customer: "But if it costs twenty dollars to make these watches, and you sell them for twenty dollars, where does your profit come in?"

Shopkeeper: "That comes from repairing them."

顾客："可是，如果这些手表的成本是二十美元，卖价也是二十美元，你怎么赚钱呢？"

店主："靠修手表赚钱呀。"

(310)

Sometimes the use of a diplomatic method defeats its own purpose, as in the case of the old fellow who was enthusiastic in praise of the busy lawyer from whose office he had just come, after a purely social call.

"That feller, for a busy man," he declared earnestly, "is one of the pleasantest chaps I ever did meet. Why, I dropped in on him jest to pass the time o´ day this mornin´, an´ I hadn´t been chattin´ with ´im more´n five minutes before he´d told me three times to come and see ´im agin."

有时候客套会适得其反。比如有这么一位老先生，在对一位事务繁忙的律师进行了一次纯礼节性的拜访之后，啧啧地称赞道：

"那位先生，"他发自内心地说，"是我见过的最讨人喜欢的大忙人。这不，我去他那里只是为了打发早晨那点时间，可是，我才和他说了不到五分钟的话，他就连说了三次让我再去看他。"

(311)

An eminent doctor successfully attended a sick child. A few days later, the grateful mother called on the physician. After expressing her realization of the fact that his services had been of a sort that could not be fully paid for, she continued:

"But I hope you will accept as a token from me this purse which I myself have embroidered."

The physician replied very coldly to the effect that the fees of the physician must be paid in money, not merely in gratitude, and he added:

"Presents maintain friendship; they do not maintain a family."

"What is your fee?" the woman inquired.

"Two hundred dollars," was the answer.

The woman opened the purse, and took from it five $100 bills. She put back three, handed two to the discomfited physician, then took her departure.

一位名医治好了一个生病的小孩儿。几天之后，满怀感激之情的母亲前来拜访医生。在千恩万谢、说自己无论如何也报答不了他的恩情之后，她说：

"可是，为了表示感谢，我希望你能接受这个钱包，这是我亲手绣的。"

医生冷冷地表示看病的费用必须用钱支付，仅仅表示感谢是不够的，然后，他又补充道：

"礼物可以维系友谊，却不能维系一个家庭。"

"那医疗费是多少？"女人问。

回答是："两百美元。"

女人打开钱包，从里面拿出五张 100 美元的钞票，取出三张，把其余两张递给尴尬不已的医生，然后转身离去。

(312)

"You know you should love your neighbor as yourself."

"But the trouble is, when I try to do that, I always end by hating myself."

"你应该像爱自己一样爱你的邻居。"

"可问题是，我那样做的时候，最后总是要恨我自己。"

(313)

There has been much controversy for years as to the proper definition of the much abused word "gentleman." Finally, by a printer´s error in prefixing to an adverb, an old and rather mushy description of a gentleman has been given a novel twist and a pithy point. A contributor´s letter to a metropolitan daily appeared as follows:

"Sir—I can recall no better description of a gentleman than this—"

"'A gentleman is one who never gives offense unintentionally.'"

绅士一词多年来一直被人们滥用，而且关于它的确切定义，一直存在很大争议。终于，由于一位印刷工的工作失误，在副词前加上了错误的前缀，从而一改人们对绅士一词陈旧、模糊的理解，而赋予其新的意义和明确的含义。以下是一个投稿人给《都市日报》写的信：

"先生——对绅士的描述，我再也想不起比下面这个更好的了——

"绅士就是从来不不故意冒犯别人的人。

（注：本来应该是：绅士就是从来不故意冒犯别人的人。Intentionally 前面错误地加上了 un，于是变成了 unintentionally 不故意）"

(314)

Wife: "My dear, we've simply got to change our family doctor. He's so absent-minded. Why, this afternoon he was examining me with his stethoscope, and while he was listening he called out suddenly, 'Halloa! Who is it speaking?'"

妻子："亲爱的，我看我们不能再用这个家庭医生了。他太心不在焉了。今天下午他在用听诊器给我检查身体的时候，突然叫起来'喂，请问是哪位？'"

(315)

During the siege of Paris in the Franco-German war, when everybody was starving, one aristocratic family had their pet dog served for dinner. The master of the house, when the meal was ended, surveyed the platter through tear-dimmed eyes, and spoke sadly:

"How Fido would have enjoyed these bones!"

德法战争期间，德军包围了巴黎。那个时候所有的人都忍受着饥饿的煎熬。有一个贵族家庭，不得不将他们的宠物狗摆上了晚餐餐桌。饭毕，主人泪眼模糊地望着汤盘中的骨头，无比悲伤地说：

"大骨头是我们的爱犬肥嘟的最爱呀！"

(316)

What true friendship consists in depends on the temperament of the man who has a friend. It is related that at the funeral of Mr. Scroggs, who died extremely poor, the usually cold -blooded Squire Tightfist was much affected.

"You thought a great deal of him, I suppose?" some one asked him.

"Thought a great deal of him? I should think I did. There was a true friend. He never asked me to lend him a cent, though I knew well enough he was starving to death."

什么是真正的友谊，因人而异。据说，斯库罗格先生在贫病交加之中死去之后，在葬礼上，平时冷血成性的吝啬鬼乡绅非常伤心。

"您一定很怀念他吧？"有人问。

"很怀念他？那当然，他是个真正的朋友。虽然就快饿死了，虽然我很清楚他当时的境况，但他始终没开口找我借过一分钱。"

(317)

She: "Have you heard anything about the woman's Reform Club?"

"Yes, its object seems to be to reform everything except the Club and everybody

except the members."

她："你听说 '妇女变革俱乐部' 的事情了吗？"

"听说了，她们的目标好像就是要变革一切事，但是不包括俱乐部；她们还要改造所有人，但不包括俱乐部成员。"

（318）

The amiable old lady was overheard talking to herself as she left the church along with the crowd that had attended the services:

"If everybody else would only do as I do, and stay quietly in their seats till everyone else has gone out, there would not be such a crush at the doors."

在教堂做完弥撒出来，一位温和谦让的老太太自言自语地说：

"如果大家都像我一样，等其他人都出去了，再离开自己的座位，门口肯定就不会这么拥挤了。"

(319)

Officer (drilling recruits): Hey, you, in case of fire, what do you do?

Recruit: I yell.

Officer: Yell what?

Recruit: Why, what do you suppose? Cease firing.

消防官（正在训练新入伍的消防员）：嗨，你，如果有大火，你该怎么做？

新兵：我大喊。

消防官：你喊什么？

新兵：啊？你不知道吗？停火！

(320)

In former times, when royalties were more important, a lady at a court ball was intensely gratified when a prince selected her as a partner. She was almost overwhelmed with pride when he danced a second measure with her.

"Oh," she gushed, as she reposed blissfully in his arms, "your highness does me too great honor."

The prince answered coldly:

"But no, madam. Merely, my physician has directed me to perspire."

早些时候，皇室家族比现在要尊贵得多。在一次宫廷舞会上，一位女士受邀与王子共舞，她简直受宠若惊。当王子又与她共舞第二曲的时候，女士自豪激动的心情难以自持，她依偎在王子怀里脱口而出："殿下，您对我太好了。"

王子淡淡地回答道：

"夫人，您千万别这么想。我这么做，全是因为我的医生说，我得想法子让自己出汗。"

(321)

The lady of uncertain age simpered at the gentleman of about the same age who had offered her his seat in the car.

"Why should you be so kind to me?" she gurgled.

"My dear madam, because I myself have a mother and a wife and a daughter."

电车上，一位绅士将座位让给了一位女士。于是，这位看不出年龄的女士便冲着这位似乎与她年龄相仿的男士咯咯地傻笑道：

"您怎么对我这么好？"

"亲爱的夫人，因为我也有母亲，妻子和女儿。"

(322)

The gentleman at the party, who was old enough to know better, turned to another guest, who had just paused beside him:

"Women are fickle. See that pretty woman by the window? She was smiling at me flirtatiously a few minutes ago and now she looks cold as an iceberg."

"I have only just arrived," the other man said. "She is my wife."

晚会上,一位年已不惑的绅士,对走到他身旁的一个男客人说:

"女人真是善变。看见窗边的那个漂亮女人了吗?几分钟前,她还冲我媚笑,可是此刻看上去却冷若冰霜。"

男客人说,"我刚到,她是我妻子。"

(注:know better 的意思是足够聪明,而不会做某些事情,所以,在这里翻译成"不惑"。)

(323)

The meek-looking gentleman arose hastily and offered his seat in the car to the self-assertive woman who had entered and glared at him. She gave him no thanks as she seated herself, but she spoke in a heavy voice that filled the whole car:

"What are you standing up there for? Come here, and sit on my lap."

The modest man turned scarlet as he huskily faltered:

"I fear, madam, that I am not worthy of such an honor."

"How dare you!" the woman boomed. "You know perfectly well I was speaking to my niece behind you."

公共汽车上，进来一位盛气凌人的女士。在她的灼灼目光之下，一脸谦和的男士立刻站起来将座位让给了她。女士也毫不客气地坐下，接着整个车厢都能听到她的高声喊叫：

"你站在那里干什么？到这边来，坐在我的腿上。"

那位谦逊的男士闻听此言，满脸通红，支支吾吾地说：

"夫人，我恐怕无法受此殊荣。"

"你好大胆！"女士大声呵斥道。"你明明知道，我是在对我的侄女说话，她就在你身后。"

(324)

The little man was perfectly harmless, but the lady sitting next to him in the car was a spinster, and suspicious of all males. So, since they were somewhat crowded on the seat, she pushed the umbrella between her knee and his and held it firmly as a barrier. A shower came up, and the woman when she left the car, put up the umbrella. As she did so, she perceived that the little man had followed her. She had guessed that he was a masher, now she knew it. She walked quickly down the side street, and the man pursued through the driving rain. She ran up the steps of her home, and rang the bell. When she heard the servant coming to the door, feeling herself safe at last, she faced about and addressed her pursuer angrily:

"How dare you follow me! How dare you! What do you want, anyhow?"

The drenched little man at the foot of the steps spoke pleadingly:

"If you please, ma´am, I want my umbrella."

公交车上，那个矮个儿男人一点也不可怕，可是，坐在他旁边的那位女士是个老处女，她提防所有的男性。公共汽车上比较拥挤，所以，她把自己的伞拿来挡在膝盖前，把矮个儿男人的伞紧紧地攥在手里横在他们两个之间。天开始下雨，女人撑着伞下车了。可是，她发现那个矮个儿男人也跟着下车了。她现在认定那个男人肯定不怀好意。于是，她快步如飞地沿着街边向前走，那个男人也冒着雨紧随其后。她跑上自家的台阶，摁响了门铃。听见仆人前来开门的脚步声，她觉得自己安全了，于是转过身来，对着追上来的男人大声喝道：

“你竟敢跟着我！好大的胆子！你到底想干什么？”

浑身已经湿透的矮个儿男人站在台阶下，哀求说：

“夫人，求求您，把伞还给我。”

(325)

George: “I proposed to that girl and would have married her if it hadn't been for something she said.”

Fred: “What did she say?”

George: “No!”

乔治：“我向那个女孩儿求婚了。如果不是因为她说那种话，我本来可以和她结婚的。”

佛瑞德：“她说什么了？”

乔治：“她说‘不行’！”

(326)

It was nine o'clock in the morning, but this particular passenger on the platform of the trolley car still wore a much crumpled evening suit.

As the car swung swiftly around a curve this riotous liver was jolted off, and fell heavily on the cobble stones. The car stopped, and the conductor, running back, helped the unfortunate man to scramble to his feet. The bibulous passenger was severely shaken, but very dignified.

"Collision?" he demanded.

"No," the conductor answered.

"Off the track?" was the second inquiry.

"No," said the conductor again.

"Well!" was the indignant rejoinder. "If I´d known that, I wouldn´t have got off."

时间已是早晨 9 点钟,可是,有轨电车上一位乘客还穿着晚礼服。他站在电车平台上,浑身皱皱巴巴,样子很是特别。

电车来了个大转弯，一下子把这个酒意仍酣的乘客给甩了出去，他重重地落在了铺着鹅卵石的路面上。电车立刻停了下来,售票员跑过来,把这个倒霉的家伙扶了起来。这一惊吓非同小可,可是醉汉仍然保持着起码的尊严。

"撞车了?"他质问道。

"没有。"售票员回答。

"脱轨了?"他接着质问。

"没有。"售票员接着回答。

"什么!"醉汉异常愤怒。"早知道是这样,我就不下车了。"

(327)

The very convivial gentleman left his club happy, but somewhat dazed. On his homeward journey, he ran against the vertical iron rods that formed a circle of protection for the trunk of a tree growing by the curb. He made a tour around the barrier four times, carefully holding to one rod until he had a firm grasp on the next. Then, at last, he halted and leaned despairingly against the rock to which he held, and called aloud for succor:

"Help! help! Somebody let me out!"

一个非常喜欢喝酒的绅士从俱乐部走了出来,很兴奋,但是,有点醉醺醺了。回家的路上,路边一棵树的围栏挡住了他的去路。这个围栏是用笔直的铁栏杆围成的。醉汉一个栏杆一个栏杆挨个摸着,足足摸了四圈。最后,他终于停下来,绝望地抓着一个栏杆,大声喊道:

"救命呀!救命呀!快来人放我出去!"

(328)

The highly inebriated individual halted before a solitary tree, and regarded it as intently as he could, with the result that he saw two trees. His attempt to pass between these resulted in a near-concussion of the brain. He reeled back, but presently sighted carefully, and tried again, with the like result. When this had happened a half-dozen times, the unhappy man lifted up his voice and wept.

"Lost—Lost!" he sobbed. "Hopelessly lost in an impenetrable forest!"

一个醉汉在一棵树前停了下来，集中目力去看这棵树。结果呢，树在他眼里变成了两棵。他试图从这两棵树之间穿过去，结果却撞了脑袋。他踉踉跄跄地后退了几步，又认真地看了看，又试了一次，结果还是撞了头。这样折腾了六次，这个痛苦的人扯开嗓子哭了起来。

"迷路了——迷路了！无法穿越的大森林！我迷路了！"